Endorsements for *Through the Storm*

"An important, insightful, and compelling read for leaders at every level guiding their organizations through adversity and looking for thoughtful tactics, techniques, and procedures for doing so. Travis Hearne's *Through the Storm* provides a tremendous examination of what it takes to lead in the face of the greatest imaginable challenges—including combat in Iraq and Afghanistan—and it provides superb insights on how to lead competently and well in such situations."

—General David Petraeus
US Army (Ret.), former Commander of the Surge in Iraq, US Central Command, and Coalition Forces in Afghanistan; former Director of the CIA; and co-author of the *New York Times* bestselling book *Conflict: The Evolution of Conflict From 1945 to Ukraine.*

"*Through the Storm* is a no-fluff manual on leadership from someone who's been through hell and back. Dr. Hearne delivers straight talk on navigating the toughest challenges with the kind of grit and integrity you rarely see. If you want to lead like a Marine and tackle adversity head-on, this book is your playbook. It's not about fancy theories; it's about real-world lessons from someone who's led on the front lines and in the boardroom."

—Jason Miller
CEO and chairman, Strategic Advisor Board and SABx Media, international bestselling author

"Travis embodies the essence of resilient leadership. His leadership experiences, from high-stakes environments in Iraq and Afghanistan to strategic positions in cybersecurity and national security, demonstrate his capability to navigate through adversity. As the founder of

Titanium Leadership, Travis has dedicated himself to empowering leaders and organizations, showcasing his passion for leadership excellence. His life's work makes him uniquely equipped to inspire and guide others in overcoming challenges and achieving success."

—Jon Macaskill
Retired Navy SEAL Commander | LinkedIn Top Voice | Keynote Speaker | Podcast Cohost/Producer | Founder and CEO of Macaskill Consulting | Mental Health Advocate

"Great leaders constantly seek counsel and hunger for practical and tested tools for the establishment and sustainment of truly transformational culture. With a unique perspective through very different lenses of experience in the military, civilian intelligence, and Fortune 100 corporate roles, Travis Hearne serves as a guide "through the storm" of leadership in many forms. Exploring the burdens, privileges, joys, and consequences of leading people, this book offers insight to equip readers to transcend 'management' and 'supervision" to inspiring, challenging leadership of those entrusted to our care. And most of all, it is about resilience, using the fuel of failure to power our eventual success, and the willingness to plow through adversity "for the good of the herd."

—Jay Denton
Senior Vice President, Global Partner Executive, TD Synnex

"Travis leverages all of his experiences and heritage to share how to be a great leader during troubling times. The lessons learned are invaluable and his entertaining writing style makes it a great read. Leadership skills are in demand and this is a foundational tool."

—Scott Stout
Security Chief Revenue Officer, Cisco

Through the Storm

The Path to Becoming a Resilient Leader

Dr. Travis Hearne, EdD

ISBN: 979-8-89079-173-3 (hardcover)
ISBN: 979-8-89079-174-0 (paperback)
ISBN: 979-8-89079-175-7 (ebook)
ISBN: 979-8-89079-176-4 (audiobook)

TABLE OF CONTENTS

Foreword: by Mark "Oz" Geist vii

Introduction ix

SECTION 1: THE STORMS OF COMBAT LEADERSHIP

Chapter 1.   The Storm of Failure (Part 1):
The Greatest Teacher 3

Chapter 2.   The Storm of Failure (Part 2):
Changing the Outcomes. 15

Chapter 3.   The Storm of Success: There's Always
Something to Learn 29

Chapter 4.   The Storm of Leading from the Front
(Part 1): Operation Phantom Fury 43

Chapter 5.   The Storm of Leading from the Front
(Part 2): Operation Phantom Fury,
A New Mission 59

Chapter 6.   The Storm of Moral Courage: A Story of
Mental Health and Impossible Decisions. . . 74

Section 1 Conclusion: Storms of Serving Your Country . 89

SECTION 2: THE STORMS OF THE BUSINESS WORLD

Chapter 7.   Through the Storm of Creating and
             Maintaining Culture: Transformation
             and GRIT 95

Chapter 8.   Through the Storm of Seeing the
             Long Game: Opening a Hotel in 2020 . . 110

Chapter 9.   Through the Storm of Change:
             Navigating the Remote Work Revolution . . . 126

Chapter 10. The Storm of Radical Commitment:
             Thriving Through the Crash of 2008 137

Conclusion 151
About the Author 155

FOREWORD

The United States Marine Corps knows a thing or two about leadership. While I never had the privilege of serving with Travis in the Marines, as a fellow Marine Corps Veteran, former Chief of Police, and a member of the annex security team that fought to save American lives in the Battle of Benghazi, Libya, from September 11 to September 12, 2012, I understand what it means to lead teams and make sacrifices. I've faced every one of the leadership storms that Travis refers to in this book, and what Travis has uncovered in his work is a blueprint for how to move through leadership storms in a healthy way.

Travis, as a Doctor of Education in Organizational Change and Leadership, Marine Corps Combat Veteran, former leader in the intelligence community, and current corporate world leader, knows what he's talking about. Yes, the decades of leadership experience in environments that the majority of the world has never experienced qualifies him to write the book, but he would say that overcoming failures is what makes him valuable. He is a humble, honest, tough, tried, and true leader of leaders.

This world needs better leaders now more than ever—plain and simple. Throughout my career, I've seen the best and worst of leadership. What Travis is bringing into the leadership space are tangible tools to create the kind of leaders we want our children to work for. Leaders who charge through storms instead of going around them. Leaders who make others better because they are in the storm with them. Leaders with thick enough skin to face criticism and failure and continue to progress and move forward. Travis and I have had so many talks about what makes a good leader, and those conversations have made it into this book.

I know Travis's story. I know the storms he's had to face to get to where he is today, and there is no better person to write this book. His faith in the process, in learning, in passing along his knowledge, and his faith in the Lord our God is a refreshing change to the leadership world. His previous book, *Hybrid: A Guide for Successfully Leading On-Site and Remote Teams*, put him on the map as an author and expert to look out for. But his new book, *Through the Storm: Lessons from Resilient Leaders*, will re-write the literal book on leadership. My time on the battlefield, in Benghazi, as a Marine, as the Chief of Police, and as the CEO of a non-profit that helps Veterans and first responders has equipped me with the ability to identify good leadership. What Travis is doing with *Through the Storm* will create the kind of leaders I want my kids to follow and become. Buckle up. This is a journey worth taking.

Mark "Oz" Geist
Bestselling co-author of *13 Hours: The Inside Account of What Really Happened in Benghazi*

As a security and military consultant, Geist is credited with saving twenty-five people in the attack on Benghazi.

INTRODUCTION

First and foremost, well done! You have made an investment in yourself, your families, your teams, and everyone you come in contact with. The storms we are about to go through together will help you become a better and more resilient leader. They will help you lead through failure and success, teach you how to lead from the front, maintain your integrity, and overcome outrageous odds in the most difficult times. I hope that when you pass this book to a friend, put it down on your coffee table or in your library, or even donate it to a bookstore, you will have been inspired by stories of resilience and feel more confident in your ability to lead through any storm life throws your way.

What is a resilient leader, and how do we become resilient? Being resilient doesn't mean you have triumphed in every situation. It doesn't mean you knuckle down and plow through leadership issues without regard for the learning process. Resiliency is understanding storms will come and using the skills you possess and the team around you to persevere through the storm. It's a certain stick-to-it-ness that keeps leaders on track as things are devolving around them. It's preparing for the storm before it ever comes. In a recent interview with General David H. Petraeus, he told me, "Luck is what happens when preparation meets opportunity." Stories of resiliency, like the ones we are about to talk about, are all about becoming better leaders and people through and on the other side of leadership storms.

Good quality leaders change the world for the better. I've seen it happen through combat operations in Iraq and Afghanistan as a United States Marine, as an intelligence officer for the Defense Intelligence Agency preventing Islamic terrorists from attacking the United States, as a leader of a global team for a Fortune 100 company and entrepreneur, and as a husband, father, son, and brother. We are about to embark on a journey through the storms that leaders will undoubtedly face as they lead people, organizations, and, most importantly, themselves.

Throughout this journey, we will dive deep into real-world leadership storms learned from times of failure, success, grief, and change. These are things leaders face every day. These lessons were often times learned through failure, which, in my opinion, is the greatest teacher of all time. However, if I limited this work to only my experiences, I would be doing you a disservice. As an academic leadership guy and former intel nerd, I knew this book had to come with a few more sources of data; otherwise, it would have been incomplete.

Over the last five years, I've had the honor of interviewing some of the most impressive and respected leaders in the United States, who have braved some of the toughest storms a leader can encounter—the second battle of Fallujah, Iraq (Operation Phantom Fury), the economic crash of 2008, and so much more. The lessons I've learned from these fantastic individuals painted a complete picture of how to lead through the toughest storms we face in leadership and are represented in each chapter of this book.

Throughout our journey through the storm, I want you to think of a few things and ask yourself a few questions. What storms have you faced in your life that you were unprepared for? Have you ever been knocked off your metaphorical horse and felt like you couldn't get back up? Have you ever wondered how other leaders seem to blaze through leadership challenges without ever breaking a sweat? Or have you experienced the exact opposite and encountered someone who has crumbled under the immense pressure that comes with leading well?

Leadership storms are challenges leaders face that have the potential to destroy us mentally, physically, emotionally, and spiritually. Together, through each chapter of this book, we will learn how to thrive through the storms of leadership and prepare for the inevitable storms that are to come.

Why the Buffalo?

The buffalo, or the American Bison for those of you keeping score, is a herd animal, which means it spends its life in a family-like unit, mating, raising young, and protecting the rest of the herd from the harsh threats of the wild. After years of studying the buffalo's history, biology, and zoology, I learned something that inspired me.

When dangerous storms begin to brew over the horizon, most herd animals, and even humans, tend to take cover or move away from the storm—but not the buffalo. She's a different sort of animal. Instead of running for cover, the buffalo will gather its herd, take a few last bites of whatever food is near, and head directly toward the storm. The herd moves in a calculated and deliberate way, each animal taking turns facing the storm on the periphery to protect the more vulnerable from the harsh weather. As the herd moves through the storm, its remarkably thick skin, developed over eons, protects it from frigid temperatures. Its massive head clears the path and finds food, and it eventually makes it out on the other side, having shortened the amount of time the herd spends in the storm and having learned lessons on how to better brave the next one. I don't know if this instinct is lodged somewhere in the buffalo cerebral cortex, formed by thousands of years of experience of charging through storms, but that's just what they do—and it's the best example of leadership I've ever heard.

Their knack for survival, among other things, is what makes the buffalo such an amazing metaphor for leadership. However, the buffalo means something more to me on a much deeper level. My bloodline goes back to the original people of what is now the United States, the Cherokee Nation. From listening to my great-grandmother speak about her experiences and the stories she heard growing up, even after the European colonization, my Cherokee ancestors were a thriving nation in what's now known as the states of Alabama, Georgia, Tennessee, and North Carolina. The buffalo was a critical part of the Cherokee way of life. Our people relied on the buffalo for food, warmth, clothing, tools, shelter, and ceremony. The importance of the buffalo has transcended generations and has been passed on to me.

Leaders today face challenges that the leaders of the past never faced. We are moving into a critical time in our nation and economy where leaders will be tested like never before. Storms of mental health, leading hybrid and remote teams, loneliness, hiring and firing, organizational change, and so much more are all part of the life of a leader. This book will give leaders and followers alike a playbook for successfully thriving through the storms of leadership.

This journey we are about to take will uncover some hard things that you may have to face in your life. Without a doubt, we will uncover a weakness or two (or maybe even ten) and figure out ways to take these weaknesses and turn them into opportunities for growth. We will also help you identify and pull out your strengths, enhance them in ways you never thought possible, and use those strengths to take you and your people to new heights and new levels of health and success.

Throughout my working life, I've had the privilege of walking people through some of the worst storms a leader can face. I have experienced catastrophic failure, wild success, and everything in between, but the one thing that has always been true is this: Leadership storms will come, and they will keep coming, relentless at times, and as if they will never end. If we let them, these storms will destroy our motivation for success, our fervor for leading, and our overall health. As leaders, we are measured by the storms we endure and how we come out on the other side.

One of the greatest leaders of our time, Dr. Martin Luther King, stated in his book *Strength to Love* that "the ultimate measure of a man is not where he stands in the moments of comfort and convenience but where he stands at times of challenge and controversy."[1] When we encounter times of challenge and controversy in our lives, we tend to fall back on what we have seen or done in the past. Cognitively, when our brains are faced with the uncomfortable, we move into a varied state of fight or flight where we must rely on the most basic instincts to survive. This is the brain's way of keeping us safe and inside our comfort zone. The good news is that this reflex can be modified, and new outcomes can emerge where we choose to face what's in front of us rather than run away.

As a United States Marine, I relied heavily on instincts and training to get me through times of crisis and chaos. In Iraq and Afghanistan, there was often no choice but to let my training do the driving, as my cognition had to take a back seat. Lives depended on my ability to think without thinking and to use the tools I was trained in well—mainly an M240G machine gun, an M4 assault rifle, and my computer. I was proficient with each one of these tools and could always rely on the repetition of training to increase that proficiency.

---

[1]   Dr. Martin Luthor King, Strength to Love (1963, pg. 26)

Lieutenant General Victor H. Krulak spoke so eloquently on this topic, stating, "Being ready is not what matters. What matters is winning after you get there." We can be ready for the storm, but it's how we blaze a trail of excellence through that storm that truly matters.

Leading teams in the intelligence community and then in the corporate world required a different level of finesse, but the process by which I became proficient stayed the same. Repetition and training eventually transformed me from a knuckle-dragging leader of Marines into a leader within the civilian intelligence community and then a leader in the business world—three *very* separate environments, stylistically and physically. Leadership storms took a completely different form. I went from leadership storms that consisted of firefights and lives lost to storms of organizational change, firing, hiring, success, emotional health, and so much more. The storms were different, but the foundational principles of thriving through these storms were relatively the same.

So, how do we train ourselves to thrive through the storms of crisis, chaos, or even amazing success? How do we, as leaders, work through these storms and come out on the other side, having thrived instead of broken down, succeeded instead of failed, and lived instead of died? Leading other human beings is one of the hardest jobs on the planet. It is not for the faint of heart or for those unwilling to learn. So, how do we, who have chosen the life of a leader, embrace and brave the storms to come? I say we take a few lessons from the buffalo or American bison for those keeping score.

I invite you to come on this journey with me. Over the last five years, I've interviewed and polled thousands of leaders across every industry and have collected solutions to some of the most common and challenging leadership storms. Each chapter of this book will take you deep into the storm and give you tangible tools to come out on the other side healthier, stronger, smarter, and better prepared for the next one. Taking lessons learned from the buffalo, we will learn how to thicken our skin and charge through these storms with wild vigor, courage, strength, health, and confidence. Leadership is hard, but it's much harder without a strong herd that's willing to charge alongside you. As a herd, let's dive into these lessons together and learn how to thrive through any storm.

SECTION 1

THE STORMS OF COMBAT LEADERSHIP

1

THE STORM OF FAILURE (PART 1): THE GREATEST TEACHER

In high school, I had to take the American College Test (ACT) four times to get the minimum score to get into a state college and play Division 1 baseball. Each time, getting myself to the testing center became harder because I could never reach that magic number I needed to get into college and play ball. I would study hard and do all of the practice tests. Heck, I even hired a tutor to help me with the exam. I was exhausted, but I knew what I wanted. I was dead set on playing baseball in college; this test was the gateway to that dream.

By the fourth time, my dad had to push me out of bed, drag me into the car, and walk me into the testing center. I thought, *If I can't even get a high enough score on this test to get into college, how in the world will I pass a college-level course?* My confidence was a bit shaken, but I was still determined to pass this thing, and somehow, on that fourth attempt, I got the score I needed to get into college and play ball. A few anxious weeks after I took the test, I was elated when I got my scores in the mail. My parents' dreams of me leaving the house were actually going to come true, and I gained a new sense of confidence. I may have failed the first three times I tried, but with a resilient mindset, I passed and was onto the glory of college baseball.

Failure is an extremely important part of success. It creates leadership scars that have fully healed and act as a great reminder of the lessons we learned on the path to success. In my humble yet confident opinion, you cannot fully succeed without knowing the sting of failure. I, unfortunately, had to learn this the hard way and in an environment where failure has the highest stakes—human life. Often, there is no turning back from this kind of failure. And boy, did I fail hard, but not in the way you would think.

It was the spring of 2007, near the pristine beaches of Marine Corps Base Camp Pendleton, California. A chiseled, steely-eyed, young Marine lance corporal named Travis Hearne (yeah, that's me) was about to check into his first duty station, 1st Light Armored Reconnaissance (LAR) Battalion. He was ready to take on the world. I'm hoping you are picking up on a bit of sarcasm here. This is a better description of how I felt than actual reality.

First LAR was strategically situated between the Pacific Ocean's crashing waves and the rolling hills of beautiful Camp Flores, one of the smaller camps on the sprawling base of Camp Pendleton. If the wind blew just right, you could either smell the salty breeze coming off the Pacific Ocean or the gunpowder from the closest live fire range. Personally, both were rather pleasant. In my mind, I hit the jackpot for my first duty station. I was both wrong and right.

The passenger van dropped me off at the barracks, and I was told to check in with the sergeant on duty for my room assignment. I did as I was told and approached an intimidatingly crusty sergeant sitting behind the desk on the main floor of the barracks. It was a Friday afternoon, and this poor soul had the incredible misfortune of being on duty on a Friday. To say that he didn't really want to answer any questions from a boot (brand new) lance corporal was a drastic understatement. I reported in and signed the forms, and he literally threw me the keys to room 206. I'm not sure he ever looked up from his cover, but I didn't care. I was finally here. I had made it through three months of boot camp, two months of basic Marine Corps training, nine months of my Military Occupational Specialty (MOS), and other training as required as an intelligence specialist at an infantry unit. It had been, or at least I thought it had been, a tough road on the path to getting to 1st LAR, but I was here and ready for whatever was thrown my way.

I dropped my gear in room 206 and prepared to check in with the battalion's leadership. I would meet my new bosses, our battalion leadership team, and the Marines I would be working with here. I had about thirty minutes before the battalion went on liberty for the weekend, so I had to hurry. I threw on my dress Alphas, which is the Marine Corps uniform required for special events and checking into a new unit, quickly shined my corframs, straightened my ribbon and shooting badge (yes, singular ribbon), and sprinted into the headquarters building where I would sit and wait for our lieutenant colonel to call me into his office.

After about ten minutes of sitting at the position of attention, a staff sergeant yelled at me from another room, "Hearne, get the hell in here! What in the world are you doing next to the battalion commander's office? You were supposed to be in here ten minutes ago." I *didn't* know that only Marine Corps officers checked in with the battalion commander. As a lowly lance corporal, I was to check in directly with the intel shop. So, I fumbled my paper orders back into my record book and sprint-walked toward the intel shop on the opposite side of the building. I jolted through the door and stood at attention in front of the senior intelligence officer and my new boss,

Staff Sergeant (SSgt) Brewster. I was sweaty, and my awkward shuffle down the hall and across the building made my uniform a complete mess—great first impression.

"What in the world were you thinking, Lance Corporal Hearne? Who told you to bother the CO (commanding officer) with your presence? Do you even know what time it is?"

I responded the only way I knew how: "Yes, staff sergeant!"

In the room across the hall were the other intelligence Marines assigned to the unit with whom I would get intricately acquainted over the next year and a half—another lance corporal, a corporal, and a sergeant. I rounded out this bunch of ragtag intel dudes. I could hear the Marines across the hall whispering but couldn't make out what they were saying; however, SSgt Brewster's voice was coming in loud and clear. "Give me your orders and service records before I decide to make you stand here until Monday," he sternly mumbled.

It was 1630, and I was getting in the way of the first sip of a frosty cold brew after a hard week of training. "Looks like you are pretty decent at physical training and not too stupid. I can probably work with that, but you better be every bit as motivated as your record shows. I don't have time to shine up another turd to babysit in Iraq once we get there."

I quickly learned that our battalion was heading to Iraq in four months and had arrived *just* in time for the pre-deployment training to begin. Most other Marines in the intelligence shop had just returned from Iraq six months earlier. Not only that, but SSgt Brewster was about to deploy to Iraq for the fifth time. This would be his first deployment as an intel Marine. Prior to 1st LAR, SSgt Brewster was an infantryman and prior security forces. Yes, he was a badass, and I didn't know it at the time, but Michael Brewster would become one of the best mentors and friends I had in the Corps.

As he finished up with my record book, he calmed down a bit, leaned back in his chair, and took a breath. "Okay,

Hearne. Next week, we kick off our pre-deployment training cycle. What that means is tomorrow, we head to Red Beach for the Highlander games. After that, the suck begins, but tomorrow night, we celebrate."

After giving him a puzzled look, he stopped me before I could ask. "Stop thinking so hard. You will hurt yourself. The Highlander games are a part of our battalion heritage. We are the *1st LAR Highlanders*, so before we head off to battle, we celebrate and indulge in a kick-ass evolution of training. Tomorrow at 1300, we hike three miles to the beach, where we partake in a series of primitive Highlander games and good old-fashioned debauchery. We will drink beer, eat pigs that have been roasted in the ground, watch some of our leaders ground fight until one Marine remains, and sleep under the stars. It's gonna be a hoot, so get your gear ready and get some sleep. I'll see you back here with all of your gear at 1200." So, I did just that.

The next day, I took the short walk from my barracks room to the headquarters building and joined the rest of H&S company. Our leadership team inspected our gear, making sure we had everything we needed for the day and evening campout. After my gear was inspected and I knew I had everything I needed, I glanced out the window at the parade deck, which is basically an empty parking lot between two barracks buildings. What I saw gave me chills—about nine hundred battle-hardened, salty-browed Marines standing loosely in formation, ready to have the time of their lives, even if it was only for one night. I had never seen that many Marines at once.

"That's an entire battalion of Marines prepping for war in Highlander fashion," SSgt Brewster proudly stated, watching from the window of our office space.

Let me unpack how a Marine Corps battalion is constructed. There are several support Marines within an infantry battalion. They aren't trained as infantry, but their jobs often cross over while deployed. Intel guys are used as machine gunners, and cooks are trained as combat medics. Every Marine is, indeed, a rifleman—especially at 1st LAR. Let me give you a quick down-and-dirty look at how our battalion was organized.

Within 1st LAR battalion were five companies with around two hundred Marines in each company, so a battalion of Marines in 2007 was about one thousand—give or take a few dozen. You had the infantry companies Alpha, Bravo, Charlie, and Delta. Then, you had the Headquarters and Service (H&S) company, which was made up of five separate sections. The admin section (S1) kept everything running administratively; the intel section (S2) supplied the companies within the battalion with the battlefield intelligence necessary to accomplish the mission; the operations section (S3) acted as the planning and action arm of the unit; the logistics and supply section (S4) gave the Marines in the battalion the gear and equipment they needed to get the job done, and finally, the communications section (S6) was responsible for all the electronic communications and computer gear. I was the newest Marine in the intelligence section of H&S company. All of us together made up a part of the greatest fighting force the world has ever seen.

Once H&S company was all accounted for and all our gear was inspected, we joined the rest of the battalion out on the parade deck. We quickly lined up in our designated spot among our fellow Highlanders and waited anxiously for our Battalion Commander to walk out of the headquarters building and lead us to Red Beach. It felt a bit like I'd won one of Willy Wonka's golden tickets and was waiting for Willy to grace the crowd with his presence before escorting the lucky winners through the chocolate factory—except in this case, Willy Wonka was a combat-hardened Marine Corps lieutenant colonel in charge of one thousand motivated oompa loompas.

Then, it happened, seemingly in slow motion. Dressed in a black and green traditional Scottish kilt accompanied by knee-high socks and Scottish sporran (a small bag worn around his waist to hold his flask), the battalion commander walked down the stairs of the headquarters building and onto the parade deck. He took his post in front of the entire battalion, looked upon a sea of desert-colored camouflaged uniforms, and nodded with a sense of quiet yet intense acceptance. This was his domain—his battalion. These were his Marines, and damn, was he proud of us.

After a few short moments, and with no discussion or dialogue needed, he shouted, "Highlanders!" Without hesitation, the entire battalion responded, "Lock shields!" a response that still rings in my ears. The sound reverberated against the barracks walls, amplifying the thousand intense voices as if they were ten thousand. It meant we were willing to lock our shield with the Marines to the right and left of us. It meant that we were willing to go to war with our brothers in arms. We were committed to one another, from the most junior private to the commanding officer. It was unlike anything I'd ever experienced before, and I'll remember it and be motivated by it until the day I die.

The Highlander games were just as SSgt Brewster explained. We hiked out to the beach, engaged in hand-to-hand combat, shared a primal meal, and bonded as brothers going into battle together should. But once they were over, it was time to get down to business. Over the next few months, we would be pushed to the max, both physically and mentally, in preparation for our deployment to Iraq. We would hike with outrageously heavy packs for dozens of miles, learn every weapon system in our arsenal, take courses to learn important Arabic phrases, and then repeat it all over again. Repetition was the name of the game, and finally, in October 2008, we made our way to Northern Iraq to begin an eight-month deployment as a part of Operation Iraqi Freedom.

The deployment to Iraq was extremely challenging, but not in the way you may think. In 2008 and 2009, Operation Iraqi Freedom (OIF) was winding down, and this would be 1st LAR's last deployment to Iraq before transitioning to Afghanistan in support of Operation Enduring Freedom. By the grace of God, in the eight months we were in Iraq, we didn't lose a single Marine and successfully turned over our area of operation to the Iraqi Army in 2009 – at least for the time being. I had been promoted while we were in Iraq, and I was now leading a small team of Marines. However, this isn't where our lesson in failure begins. Our next chapter will take us through one of the most difficult battles of the Iraq war: Operation Phantom Fury. We will dive into the hardest parts of Operation Iraqi Freedom as seen through the eyes of a Marine Corps first lieutenant leading teams of Marines through the most dangerous place on Earth at the time. So, buckle up.

Over the next few months, we reintegrated into society the best we could, with the pending Afghanistan deployment always in the back of our minds. The entire battalion took their post-deployment leave, spreading out across the country to families, friends, and celebrations with those they missed. I stayed in California with my fiancé, overindulged on cheeseburgers, and caught up on some much-needed sleep. However, all good things must come to an end, and it was no different with our leave time block. By July, we were all back in the swing of things, preparing for the next deployment to Afghanistan. We didn't know it at the time, but this trip would be nothing like Iraq. We would be tested physically, mentally, emotionally, spiritually, and any other way that we could be tested. The leadership storms that came my way would change how I led forever. Herein lies the beginning of the leadership lesson.

We were a few months into reintegration training, where the focus was on checking all the annual training boxes and qualifying with the weapon systems we would be using in Afghanistan. As an intel shop, we created cultural presentations, practiced martial arts, studied enemy tactics, and analyzed terrain on top of the above-mentioned training requirements. You know, Military nerd stuff. In about January 2010, we got word from the battalion commander, Lieutenant Colonel Scott Leonard, to prepare for Highlander Night. I couldn't have been more excited. It was like the bell sounding to kick off the first round of a twelve-round boxing match. I gathered my Marines and filled them in on the tradition I knew all too well.

Highlander Night began exactly as it did the year prior. The entire battalion hiked out to Red Beach and began to bond. The first "bonding" event was ground fighting; this time, I would get to test my skills in the pit. I had been practicing my jiu-jitsu skills over the past year or so, and I was relatively proficient in what the Marine Corps called the Marine Corps Martial Arts Program. I was now a leader of Marines, and I was ready to show them how their corporal could take care of business. As soon as we reached the shores of Red Beach, the Marine Corps gladiators selected by the company commanders began lining up—each Marine on their knees in front of the other, surrounded by martial arts instructors acting as referees for the organized violence about to occur. The entire battalion surrounded us, with each company planting their guidon - a red flag embroidered with their company callsign and logo atop an eight-foot flagpole topped with a spike - deep into the loose sand. Every Marine surrounding the pit, linked arm over shoulder, was swaying back and forth, grunting and shouting, "OOH-RAH" and "AOO!" to their respected leaders in the arena. It was as if the historic Spartans were resurrected in each of us. You could taste the energy pulsating from the sand, and it was intoxicating.

I was one of the first to hit my knees in wild anticipation for any Marine foolish enough to kneel in front of me. I watched as others paired up alongside me, strategizing about how I would tap each of them out after I was finished with whomever chose me. Then, a tall, gangly, unimposing Marine knelt in front of me. He was tall, but that was about it. He was about five inches taller than me, but we weighed about the same, which gave me the upper hand. *This guy ain't nothin' but a light snack,* I thought to myself. I looked down the line to see who I would go after once I had dispatched this guy. I had the whole thing mapped out in my head: double-team that guy, sneak up on that one, armbar, rear naked choke. I visualized my entire path to victory, or so I thought.

The instructor counted down, "3…2…1… Execute!" and I jolted after the Marine's neck like a bullet out of a gun. In my mind, it would take about six to eight seconds for me to choke him out and move on. However, probably ten to fifteen seconds later, my eyes started to slowly blink. I saw nothing but blue skies and felt two Marines under each arm pulling me backward.

"What the hell happened?" I asked in a daze.

The Marines pulled me to the side of the pit to join the rest of H&S company and laughingly let me know, "Man, you went out like a light! You drew the short straw, there, corporal."

I responded, "What in the world are you talking about? Someone must have come up from behind me—probably cheated!"

"Nope," the Marines laughed. "You were up against Corporal Jacob Leicht. He wrapped his long arms around your neck before your second knee left the ground. The guy is a stud. You never really stood a chance."

"Huh," I shrugged with a conceding bit of humility. "Guess I have a thing or two to learn from Leicht."

I watched him go from Marine to Marine, tapping each one of them out with ease all the way to the final bout. He moved like butter in a microwave around the other Marine he faced in the finals and eventually got behind him, choking him out the same way he choked me out. It was at that moment I knew I had to get to know this Marine. We wrapped up Highlander Night the next day, and on the hike back to base, I introduced myself to Corporal Leicht.

"Hey, I'm Corporal Hearne. The guy you put to sleep yesterday."

He sarcastically replied, "Which one?"

And that, as they say, was the beginning of a beautiful friendship.

Over the next few months, I learned quite a bit about Jacob. Some of the Marines in his platoon called him "Bobby," relating his accent to the old cartoon, King of the Hill, but I never took to the nickname. He was Jacob to me. We trained our Marines, swapped leadership notes, and trained as leaders together. What I learned throughout this time with Jacob humbled me and gave me a sense of admiration for the man he was. Born into an adopted family on the 4th of July, Jacob wasn't your average corporal of Marines. Two years prior, while serving with a different unit in Iraq, Jacob was severely injured in an improvised explosive device (IED) attack. He was driving an up-armored Humvee when he was hit with a five-hundred-pound roadside bomb that mangled his face and snapped both his fibula and tibia. Jacob would have to spend the next two years recovering from his injuries, but that's not why he was more than average. Throughout his recovery, he fought tooth and nail to get back onto the battlefield. He wanted to be with his Marines doing what Marines did best—fighting for freedom. His fighting spirit was unlike any I had ever come across, and after years of fighting to get back into a deployable unit, he landed with me at 1st LAR.

As the training cycle progressed, Jacob and I got close. We were in different companies, but we were all in the "suck" together, so we commiserated on the weekends and during long hikes through the hills of Camp Pendleton. I learned so much from him. Just being around him made me a better Marine, a better leader, and a better man. My Marines got to know him and his Marines, and we melded into one big, dysfunctional family. Life was good. However, as it does, time passed, and it was time to head back up to March Air Force Base and then off to Afghanistan.

2

THE STORM OF FAILURE (PART 2): CHANGING THE OUTCOMES

I n April 2010, our battalion was off to the sandbox once again. It was a different flavor of sand but still the same type of dessert and climate we were used to. We first landed in Kyrgyzstan to get used to the time change and make sure our weapons were sighted in and ready. It was our last chance for a while to shower properly and stuff ourselves before heading down to our area of operations (AO). After about a week, we all called home, skyped in with our loved ones one last time, jumped on the C17, which is a giant troop-carrying airplane, and headed to Southern Afghanistan—our home for the next eight months.

After about a month in country, we were getting used to the area, finishing our turnover with 4th LAR (the reservist unit we would be replacing), and starting to conduct combat operations to give back control of the region to the Afghan people who had been ravaged and torn apart by the Taliban for the last one hundred years. My team's job was to collect information on high-valued individuals (HVIs) and then join whatever company responsible for the area that HVI was in to snatch him up. As the human intelligence Marine in charge of hunting HVIs, I was also fortunate enough to be the machine gunner for our quick reaction force (QRF), which acted as both the extra Marines for regular combat operations and as the emergency response unit dispatched when Marines needed more firepower to help win a firefight. It was tough work with long hours and, at times, very little sleep, but I loved it.

On May 24, 2010, after only being in country for a little over a month, I turned twenty-seven years old, which is pretty ancient for a corporal of Marines. I was the grand old man of the H&S Company intel shop, or at least that's what they called me. SSgt Brewster assembled what Marines he could find, including Jacob and his Marines, in front of the company prison gym (because it looked like a prison) to present me with expensive gifts, fine delicacies, and delicious cakes. It was an old Cubs hat, socks, and an MRE coffee cake with the number twenty-seven written on it in mustard. It was everything I could have hoped for. They all knew I loved the Cubs and was a sock hoarder, so the gifts were actually perfect. We sang, ate mustard-covered cake, and then went back to our tents to pack up for the next mission.

The QRF was headed out the next morning with Alpha company to find one of the HVIs who had been evading us the entire time we'd been there, but we were sure we had him cornered this time. This guy was in charge of manufacturing the IEDs buried in every road we drove in or out on, including several that killed Marines from 4th LAR. We wanted him, and badly. So, on May 25, we headed out to hunt. We searched dozens of buildings and homes and talked to everyone we could find, but we came up dry after two days of searching. Word had gotten to him that we were looking, and he high-tailed it to Pakistan, about forty miles from our area of operation.

After coming up dry, we returned to the main combat outpost (COP) to refill our water, chow, and, most importantly, Rip It energy drinks. My Marines were tired and frustrated.

We worked hard putting together the information we needed to catch this guy, but we came up short. Motivation was low, but we were, at the very least, going to get a hot meal.

Our vehicles passed through the main checkpoint leading into the COP, and we parked them in our designated area. We grabbed all our necessary gear, dismounted, and headed to the command operations center (COC) to check in and debrief with the rest of the H&S Marines. It was a short walk, about five minutes. I told my Marines to sit outside of the COC and grab a smoke or relax for a bit while I went in and handled the business we needed to handle. I made my way up the makeshift steps, opened the old wooden door, and went over to the officer in charge of the COC. Before I could get a word out of my mouth, urgent radio chatter came in from one of the companies. "Troops in contact! Troops in contact! Requesting immediate QRF to our position!" came over the radio with almost too much static to make out. We could hear the urgency in the voice of the platoon commander. Again, "Troops in contact, request immediate QRF support to grid..."

I couldn't make out the entire grid, but I knew Jacob and his Marines were in the general vicinity of the broken grid coordinate they were giving. The COC began to sprint into action, spinning up the QRF and moving any unmanned aerial vehicle (USV) we could get into the area. Then, a few seconds after the QRF request, we heard the radio call we never wanted to hear. "Troops in contact, request immediate medivac, one Marine Angel and two Marines wounded!"

My heart sank into my stomach, and I felt sick. I recognized the Marine on the radio as Jacob's platoon commander, and I knew in my soul that this would be one of the worst days of my life.

As the COC organized the chaos happening in real time, all I could do was stand there and wait. The voices over the radio told us to hold off on the QRF and that they weren't in imminent contact but that an IED had gone off on a dismounted patrol, killing one Marine and wounding two others. Again, I waited, thinking to myself, *No, it's not Jacob. It's not him. He wouldn't have made it through everything he's made it through for this to happen.* After what seemed like hours, the medivac bird landed just north of the COP with the Marine KIA and the wounded.

I rushed over to the area to see how I could help, even though there was absolutely nothing I could do. I was in a full-out sprint to the helicopter with my gear flying everywhere. I hadn't even dropped my pack. I got about fifty yards outside of the COC when one of Jacob's Marines stopped me. "Bro, don't go over there. It's Jacob, man. He's gone."

Once again, I froze, trying to make sense of what I was hearing and seeing—trying to justify my way out of the fact that Jacob was dead. "No, he's wrong. It's someone else. It's not possible. This guy wasn't even out there with them," I mumbled under my breath. I couldn't wrap my mind around the possibility that Jacob could be gone. But, in fact, it was true. He was.

On May 27, 2010, Jacob Leicht, who was born on the fourth of July, became the 1000th servicemember to be killed in Afghanistan, killed in action by an IED. The worst part about it was that there was no enemy to be seen. No firefight to be won. Just an IED detonated from a distance that ended the life of a true American hero. I went into a quiet rage, sprinting back to the COC to collect my Marines. "This has to have been from that piece of crap we have been looking for, and we aren't going to rest until we find him. Grab your packs and get back on the truck."

So, we did. We mounted up and joined another company in search of anyone who had information about who put the IED in place. We went from village to village day after day. I was running on no sleep, no food, and very little water, and worst of all, I was running my Marines into the dirt. Three days turned into four. Four days into six, and finally, on day seven, we returned to the COP to resupply. I *yelled* at my Marines to dismount and get their asses to the COC to check in. "We have two hours before we head back out, so do whatever it is you need to do, but be back on the trucks in two hours!" I barked like an idiot. I didn't care about anything but finding out who killed Jacob. I would stop at nothing, and everyone around me was going to join in my pursuit—until I got to the COC. Regardless of my orders to my Marines, they followed me toward the COC.

I was about to walk up those same makeshift steps I had walked up a week earlier, but the world was completely different now. It would never be the same, and I had to figure out the how, when, who, and most of all, the why. Before I could take the first creaky step, the main door swung wide open, almost knocking me down. SSgt Brewster saw me coming on the camera mounted outside and stopped me in my tracks. "Travis, what the hell are you doing? Why in the world do your Marines look like that? They are starving, thirsty, and exhausted. In the state they are in, they are no good to anyone. Hell, they could actually cause a lot of damage operating in that state. Sit down!"

I almost burst into tears when Brewster called me by my first name. I knew right away that I screwed up. I looked at my Marines, who were behind me at this point, and said, "Marines, drop your gear right here and go get some chow. We aren't going anywhere anytime soon."

"Sit down, man. Look, I know you and Jacob were buddies. I also know that processing the death of another Marine is extremely difficult, but I also know that this isn't the leader I, or any of the other leaders here, have taught you to be. Tell me the truth. How are you doing with Jacob's death? This is the first time you've lost someone like this, and unfortunately, he likely won't be the last. Losing Marines never gets easy, but you can't blame yourself, or even worse, your Marines, for what happened. You aren't okay, and you are destroying your Marines. You can't lead them right now. You need to take some time and grieve. I'm going to bench you for a little while, Corporal Hearne. Get yourself to the chow hall with your Marines, and then come back here, and we'll walk through a plan."

I had failed. I failed my Marines and my unit, and I failed Jacob. I wasn't being resilient; I was being irresponsible. A resilient leader would have taken the time needed to process and grieve, allowing the people around me to do the same. A resilient leader would have checked in with the people impacted by what happened. Most of all, a resilient leader would have taken the time to prepare for the next storm instead of stagnating in the current storm. Jacob didn't teach me to lead like this. I knew better. He would have choked me out again if he had seen how I treated my people. My failure wasn't that I couldn't find the guy who killed Jacob or even that I failed to keep Jacob alive. I failed by treating my Marines as tools instead of as human beings. I was so wrapped up in my hurt that I lost sight of everything I'd been taught about leading men. That day, I promised myself and my Marines that I would never be that kind of leader again.

It's a long story, I admit. However, it's one that changed the way I lead forever. I was so overcome with fixing the problem that I forgot about my greatest asset—my people. Have you ever had your back against the wall? Have you ever been pushed to the breaking point? In Afghanistan in 2010, I realized that failure was, in fact, an option. It's not a good option, but one that absolutely happens. I was lucky that I didn't get one of my Marines hurt or, worse, killed. However, what I learned from that failure changed my world, so let's digest what I learned step by step.

How has failure impacted your professional life? I can almost guarantee it has. Have you let it change you, either for better or worse? First, I want to say that what people say is true: Failure is the greatest teacher. If you can learn from a teacher, such as failure, you can put together a playbook for success and become a resilient leader. The formula for success is rather simple: You only have to succeed more often than you fail. Being successful doesn't mean you have somehow dodged the bullets of failure. It means you have the courage to learn from your mistakes and do things differently.

Now, don't get me wrong. Failure is hard to learn from, but if you can repeatedly stand up after being knocked down by failing, you will learn some of life and leadership's most valuable lessons. Every time you stand up after the storms of failure, you become increasingly stronger, immeasurably wiser, and more resilient than before the storm. But how do we get there?

> "I've missed more than nine thousand shots in my career. I've lost almost three hundred games. Twenty-six times, I've been trusted to take the game-winning shot and missed. I've failed over and over and over again in my life. And that is why I succeed. I can accept failure; everyone fails at something. But I can't accept not trying."
>
> –Michael Jordan, The GOAT!

There are a few stages that good leaders go through when overcoming failure. While each leader responds differently, in an interview of over fifty military and private sector leaders, I found that leaders go through three distinct stages. A leader has to overcome first contact, overcome the internal voice, take action, reflect, and move forward.

21

ACTION STEPS

Stage 1: Overcoming First Contact

The first stage of leadership failure is to deny, justify, and blame others. When something has gone wrong, we get angry and confused and immediately look for someone or something to blame. If we aren't careful, we can start pointing fingers, making excuses, and trying to f ind a personal out—some way to shirk responsibility for the failure by denying that it was our fault. When we do this, as leaders, we break trust with those around us and halt any kind of productivity that could help our situation. Leaders who continue to look to blame can get so overwhelmed with trying to figure out why things went wrong that they stop working and leading altogether. When SSgt Brewster benched me, my first reaction was to deny what he was saying. In my mind, at least in that initial moment, my actions were completely justified. I was just doing what Marines do, but I was doing it all wrong.

How to Overcome First Contact: How do we get through this stage of failure? How do we move out of the denial stage? The first step is to stop. Take a big breath in, recognize the situation at hand, and breathe for a minute. Whenever I felt the weight of failure, breathing exercises were my go-to. It's incredible how a few deep breaths can clear your mind and bring you back to the present. Breathing techniques have been one of the best things that I have incorporated into my day, especially when dealing with stress. When I get hit with the realization that I have failed, I fall into a pattern of re-centering my nervous system and calming my mind. I start with a deep breath in, as deeply as possible, and just when I think I've reached my limit, I take one more quick gasp and hold it for four to five seconds, followed by a slow and very intentional exhale until I can't exhale any longer. Depending on how stressed I am, I'll repeat this process at least five times, maybe more. This process biologically reduces stress and regulates your nervous system. Take a minute or so and give it a try.

Second, we find trusted people to process with. During this stage, you need people who will tell you hard truths you won't want to hear. "Yes, you screwed this up pretty badly—not *them*, but *you*." If you aren't careful, leadership can be a lonely place. However, when you intentionally surround yourself with people who will make you a better leader and hold you accountable, you can do nothing but get better. These people will help you identify the parts of the failure that you need to take responsibility for. If you're like me and are a fan of Jocko Willink and Leif Babbin's book *Extreme Ownership*, you realize that everything is your responsibility as a leader. That doesn't mean that everything is your *fault*, but as a leader, it is your responsibility.

This group of accountability partners will be a common theme throughout this book. We can do so much more together than we can alone. Leadership is no different. During this phase, we process and analyze solutions to problems, but we begin to take ownership of the failure and resulting impacts. Understand that the world isn't ending. Nobody is being shot at (hopefully), and there is always a solution; you just have to adjust your expectations of the previously intended outcome.

Stage 2: Overcoming the Internal Voice (Self-Blame and Self-Pity)

The second stage of the failure process is to blame yourself. Now, I want to say there is a **huge** difference between blaming yourself and taking responsibility. Even if we are taking responsibility in a healthy way, good leaders blame themselves for failing and can fall into a state of micro-depression. Self-deprecating talk like, "It's all my fault," "How could I let that happen," or "I'm just not cut out for this stuff" are common themes after failure. The feeling of letting others and yourself down can be overwhelming and can destroy a leader's confidence. Once I realized what I'd done, I couldn't see past my guilt. I hated who I was at that moment and was bargaining my way out of the failure. Thoughts like, *Just move me to another unit or send me home,* popped into my head. This reaction is highly typical when we fail. We see that we played a small, medium, or large part in some sort of professional failure, and we feel guilty. It's normal; it's common, and it's okay.

Overcoming the Inner Voice: This is the stage where most leaders throw in the towel after failure—but not us. This is when we need our people most. To bring it back to the buffalo, there is a herd assembled around us to walk us through this, holding us accountable for what needs accountability, cheering us on when we start to take steps toward recovery, and helping us strategize how to get to the other side. The storm is here, and you are stuck in the middle of it.

First, in order to bring ourselves out of the fog of self-blame and micro-depression, we need to lay out the facts. What happened? When did it happen? How did it happen? What happened from that incident? Who was impacted? How can we strategize and create a plan to shift the outcome from failure to something that resembles success? Again, the original goal has flown out the window. You can't change what happened, but you *can* change how you respond, how you treat your people, and, ultimately, the outcome. Just because you failed doesn't mean that it's over. The outcome may just have to shift. Lay out all of the data and start creating a plan.

Stage 3: Take Action, Reflect, Move Forward

You failed? Okay, now what? This is the most important stage because it is the first step to creating a different outcome. Yes, sometimes there is no way to create a better outcome for some failures. Sometimes, you have to just burn the ships and start over, but rarely is there *nothing* in your control as a leader. After you've overcome and defeated the voice of self-blame and micro-depression, collected the data you need to fully understand and take responsibility for the failure, and created a mitigation strategy, it's time to implement that strategy.

Without taking action, you will have given in to your failure. This is the most important step, but this is also the most challenging step. I mean, you *just* failed! Those inner voices are likely beginning to resurface. "Don't try this again!" "You are going to screw this whole thing up again if you try this." Here's the thing. Yes, whatever you do may not work. You may fail again. In fact, there is a good chance you will. Then, it's back to the drawing board. However, if you don't try and you give in to failure, you will never know the taste of success through the storm of failure. Grab your herd and put your new strategy into play. Use your team to help move toward the edge of the storm and out the other side.

Whether your actions created a positive outcome from the failure or not, it's extremely important to reflect on the lessons you learned from the process and move forward. Learning only occurs when you are willing to dig back into a subject—in this case, the subject is a failure. Write down what you learned, the pain points, the struggles you had, and the success you saw. In most cases, there are multiple parts of failure, some of which are pieces of success. Take note of those. This is where you create your playbook for success based on your failures.

Creating a Playbook: The Failure Resume

After each failure, I put together a *failure resume*. Let me explain. This is a consolidated report of my failure. It starts with the 5Ws and an H (who, what, where, when, why, how). Writing these down accomplishes a couple of things. First, it helps you process what happened. You will remember aspects of the problem you may have missed before as you write. You may encounter a hidden treasure of success that you never thought to celebrate. Second, it gives you something to look back on when you are faced with an opportunity where you might fail. "Okay, last time I tried to hit my sales goal, I completely missed it. What happened that year? What should I do differently? What can I try this year that I didn't do last year to make sure I blow my number out of the park?" Look back at the failure resume and create a strategy of how *not* to do that again. Take the good, learn from the bad, and move forward.

Never let a failure stop you from trying. Never let failure stop you from leading. You have picked up this book because you care about leading well. That, in and of itself, is a *huge* credit to your leadership and is a big step toward moving forward. You can change your outcome by changing your mindset. Failure tends to push us into the mindset of a victim. Resilient leaders will use that mindset to their advantage, morphing the victim into the opportunity. Failure is always another opportunity to succeed.

Let's go back to my experience in Afghanistan. Two weeks later, I was back on the truck and leading my Marines in the hunt for Taliban leaders, but during that month, I walked through each one of these stages. First, I immediately started blaming others. I blamed the Taliban, my team, my leadership, and even my country (not my best moments). Once I was able to take a step back, SSgt Brewster and a few other close friends helped me take ownership of how I was treating my Marines and taking responsibility for their welfare. It was my job to take care of them and bring them home safely to their families. Then, it was on to create a strategy of reconciliation with my Marines and a plan for how we were going to move forward as a team. Through a ton of brainstorming and learning from my leaders, I was able to reconnect with my Marines and apologize for how I led, vocalize a roadmap for rebuilding trust with them, and create an operational game plan for the next five months. Jacob was gone, but that wouldn't dictate how I led my Marines any longer. Only four short months later, we would find ourselves in the middle of our battalion's most important missions, destroying a Taliban stronghold and taking back a large piece of the country for the Afghan people.

Reflecting on these failures, I realized that while failure is indeed a great teacher, what we do with these lessons truly defines us. These lessons are key to turning failure into success. If we ignore the lessons, we miss out on doing things differently later; as we move forward, the challenge lies in accepting failure and actively changing the outcomes. Through the crucible of changing outcomes, we learned that resilience is built on both success and failure. As we prepared for our next mission, we knew that success could be another storm to navigate, with its own challenges and lessons. This is where the true test of leadership begins, bringing us to our next journey: transforming failure into success.

Pictures

3

THE STORM OF SUCCESS: THERE'S ALWAYS SOMETHING TO LEARN

F ailure may be the greatest teacher, but success is by far the greatest motivator and can be just as challenging as overcoming failure. When we succeed, the brain celebrates. Feeling the rush of dopamine that floods your brain when good things happen is unlike any other experience. It's addicting! You want that feeling repeatedly and will stop at nothing to recreate it. However, sometimes, if we let it, success can lead us down a road that will end in failure.

Success isn't just an end state or a conclusion. It's a storm in and of itself. Success can blind us from the ultimate mission, inflate our ego, and make us lazy. It can lead us down a road of unabashed arrogance and, if we aren't careful, create a false sense of completion that can be detrimental to future success. Before we dig into that, let's dive into one of the biggest successes of my military career.

It was about two weeks after Jacob died that I was able to grieve a bit and get my head in a space where I could lead my Marines again. They could trust me again, and we were able to pick up where we left off. It was good to be "back on the truck." Over the past several months, my Marines and I had been on dozens of missions where the objective was clear, and the outcome was relatively predictable—extremely dangerous and difficult, but predictable, nevertheless. We would help the locals plant grain in place of poppy, hunt for Taliban fighters in tiny towns in southern Helmand Province, and confiscate and destroy narcotics coming from the south. At times, it felt eerily identical to our Iraq deployment from the previous year. Sometimes, it was hard to keep my Marines motivated. At this point, we were toward the end of our deployment, and their motivation was clear and firmly founded in whatever cheeseburger or beer they were going to overconsume as soon as we were back in sunny Southern California. However, the mission we were about to embark on was anything but predictable or routine. This would be our last operation in Afghanistan: Operation Steal Dawn. We were headed home after this, and it couldn't happen fast enough.

We had already lost three Marines, including Jacob, and were anticipating even more casualties on this particular mission. We were headed to one of the only remaining Taliban strongholds in Southern Helmand Province, and we knew we were in for a fight. The trip would take us about fifty kilometers south of our base to the Afghanistan-Pakistan border. We'd been down there a few times before, mainly just to poke the hornets' nest, but this operation was different. A small portion of our battalion, a contingent of British Royal Marines, and a fair amount of air support would destroy the Taliban's tactical capacity, cripple their explosives and narcotics operations, and take down as many of their fighters as possible. It was what we trained for, but man, would it push us out of our comfort zones. I was the senior Marine in the vehicle traveling in the convoy's rear. I had my M4 carbine and my M9 baretta pistol at my side and enough energy drinks to keep me awake for days. My primary weapon, a trusty M240G machine gun, was mounted in front of me. I had my Marines with me; they were motivated, and we were ready to go—nervous but ready to go. We headed south on a journey that would take twenty-four hours, but as we reached our first staging point just outside of the town, Mother Nature gave us an opportunity to reflect a bit.

The strangely satisfying smell of a sandstorm that has been overwhelmed by a sudden and unexpected torrential downpour is as unique an experience as there is, rivaled only by the sight of it. Watching this magnificent mountain of sand, dancing, and fighting to stay alive against an overpowering rainstorm was like watching the Almighty engage in fierce and absolute combat with the devil himself. I got a front-row seat from the turret of an MRAP All-Terrain Vehicle (M-ATV). As I sat and watched this once-in-a-lifetime event unfold, I thought to myself, *Ah, Afghanistan. I might miss you just a tiny bit.*

The fresh rain falling from the swirling black clouds was inundating the reddish-brown sandstorm billowing from the south, filling the air with an orange tint and a smell that can only be described as one of the most refreshing yet overpowering sensations one human sense can experience. It was literally raining mud. Powerful thunder and penetrating lightning overstimulated every nerve in my body. The terrain of Afghanistan had to be the only place on Earth where this phenomenon was possible, and I saw it with my US Marine Corps brothers, whom I would never forget.

My machine gun was locked to the rear, ready to take on whatever was sent my way, but our four-vehicle convoy had been halted due to the pending sandstorm and in preparation to travel through a narrow, IED-laden mountain pass. As the storm got closer to our convoy, I battened down the hatches and prepared to get pounded by the commanding sandstorm, which was nothing new. We had been stuck in dozens of sandstorms throughout the deployment but had never experienced one like this. We watched through our tiny windows as this larger-than-life scene played out in front of us, knowing that once it was safe to move, we were headed into a part of Afghanistan that very few Western militaries had ever been.

We knew that we were headed toward a firefight with the Taliban, and we knew that our route was already mapped out by the enemy and laced with IEDs. As I mentioned before, it was quite a long journey to get to our objective from our COP (combat outpost), and we had to travel over miles and miles of open desert before we reached the mountains of Southern Afghanistan. What that meant was that our large convoy of giant vehicles created tornadoes of sand on our way to our objective. The enemy saw us coming from miles away. Every vehicle we stopped on our route would let us know that we were correct in our assumption that the Taliban knew we were coming and were ready for us.

Nevertheless, after about forty-five minutes of watching and waiting, the convoy commander said it was time to move out over the radio. This meant we had about five to ten minutes before starting our journey through the rocky and treacherous mountains down a single-lane dirt "road." We had no idea what to expect. Every contingency imaginable was going through my head. How do you plan if you don't know what will happen? Questions like these can put a real damper on motivation. I could see my Marines' faces begin to fill with doubt and fear. We had been charging hard for months, and it was as if stopping, even for a moment, gave them the opportunity to really understand what we were about to do. I could tell that their motivation was decreasing, and doubt was beginning to creep in. So, I went over the operational order again, and we quickly talked about what we would do when the operation was over. Who would be in charge of refilling the vehicle with gas? Who was in charge of grabbing chow? Who would shine my boots when we got back to the FOB (that answer was me)? We answered questions that highlighted the fact that we would all make it out of this, and slowly but surely, I could see the motivation begin to stir in their spirits once again.

Our destination was one of the few remaining Taliban strongholds in Southern Helmand and throughout the entire province, and it was split by the invisible Pakistan-Afghanistan border. We had access to one road in and one road out. There was another road out of the town, but the problem with that road was that we didn't have access to it. It was in Pakistan, and we were given strict orders to stay out unless we wanted to cause an international incident. We really didn't want that to happen.

As we started checking our communication gear and made sure our ammunition was readily available, what we were about to do hit home. The unknown became doubt, which turned into fear. Would I make it home? Would my new wife receive nothing but a folded flag and a letter from a thankful nation? I felt nervous, nauseous, and scared all at once, but I couldn't show it. I wasn't anywhere near the senior Marine in the convoy, but I was the senior Marine in the vehicle, and at the very least, I had to look like I could lead my Marines and our Navy Corpsmen brother down this road. While my nerves were on the verge of getting the best of me, my face was still, and my trigger finger was ready. After checking my weapon and giving a quick and motivating "Ooh-rah" to my Marines, I sat back, closed my eyes, said a prayer, and began to visualize our plan. Our team was motivated. We had been training for this operation for months. My Marines knew the risks *and* the rewards for a job well done. We knew setbacks, delays, curveballs, and unexpected circumstances would throw us off. This storm was one of them, but it didn't matter. We had a job to do and the discipline to get it done well.

As I thought about all the potential outcomes that could play out over the next forty-eight hours, the magnitude of what my decisions could cost hit home like a bullet to the flak jacket. I looked at my Marines. I knew my main objective was to keep them disciplined, motivated, and, most of all, alive. Our unit's objective was to take over a Taliban stronghold and narcotic bazaar where poppy plants were processed into black tar heroin and exported all over the world. The narcotics that were distributed from this village were responsible for most of the drug overdoses in Europe, Russia, and Asia, accounting for thousands of deaths. Not only that, but the bazaar was also the most prolific manufacturer of homemade explosives (HME), which were responsible for killing Jacob and two of our Marines in the months prior. Many of the homemade explosives that killed Military members and Afghan civilians came from this bazaar. To say that we wanted to put an end to their people-killing business was a dramatic understatement.

Our job was, at the very least, to put a dent in their operation, but we were certain that the Taliban wasn't going down without a fight. At that moment, my personal mission was put into perspective. The reality and weight of the consequences of poor decision-making became tangible. I had to be flexible in my decision-making, able to shift my thought process and leadership style depending on what the situation called for, and rely on my discipline to carry me through.

The American military hierarchy is built upon orders and a chain of command for a reason—because it works. At that moment, I knew I could rely on that structure to lead, but at the end of the day, the structure is only as good as the leader in command of it. I had to find a fluid balance between hierarchy and humanity to get my Marines through this mountain pass and to keep my stuff together. After what seemed like days, I was jolted back into the present by the starting of my vehicle's diesel engine, smoke billowing out of the back tailpipes and into the turret in which I was mounted. The convoy commander gave the command, and we moved out, following right behind the rain.

The rain had put an end to the massive sandstorm and turned the road into a trail of thick red mud, forcing the convoy to move more slowly than we would have liked, but we pushed on toward our objective. From the turret of the last vehicle, I could see the entire countryside behind the convoy. The vast sandy desert quickly met the rocky and treacherous mountains of Southern Afghanistan, and as we headed into the mountain pass, I noticed something. Small pieces of broken wood, multicolored wires, and plastic jugs were beginning to surface on either side of our convoy. I was curiously watching and waiting for one of the vehicles to hit an IED, but it never happened.

The rain was still very heavy in front of us, making the roads a muddy mess, but not a drop fell on us. After passing the third set of what I now recognized as IED components, the convoy came to another stop. The convoy commander came over the radio asking for our explosives ordinate disposal (EOD) sergeant to dismount and figure out what was going on. The EOD sergeant knew what the pieces were immediately but agreed to investigate. We shifted the vehicles into a defensive posture and settled in for what we thought would be a while. It was still very early in the morning, before sunrise, and what I saw still gives me goosebumps to this day. As I looked through my night vision goggles (NVGs), I saw Taliban fighters in the hills—like ants moving in and out of crevasses and caves. They weren't moving into fighting positions or getting ready to attack. They were realizing, at about the same time we were, that they would have to think of another way to stop our convoy from reaching our destination.

After a few minutes of visually clearing the area for Taliban fighters, the EOD sergeant dismounted and headed toward a particular set of wires. Metal detector in hand, he swept the area for IEDs and quickly hit pay dirt. Directly under the wires and busted-up wood was a fifty-pound yellow jug of homemade explosives, which would have demolished our vehicle and every United States Marine and Navy Corpsman in it. Once he marked the jug, he moved on to investigate the wires. He opened his multi-tool, which was basically a pair of needle-nose pliers with several other attachments on it, and sorted through the mess.

When it seemed like he had conducted a thorough investigation, he quickly stood up, moved back to the truck, and jumped in the first vehicle. After only a few seconds of discussion, the convoy commander came over the radio. "The rain completely destroyed the IEDs on our path. We actually ran over three of them before we got to this one. Whoever was praying for a miracle on this operation, keep it up!"

The rain had destroyed the wood the Taliban was using as an initiator for the IEDs. I heard an audible gasp from my Marines in the vehicle, looking to me for leadership and guidance. With a renewed sense of security and a burst of confidence, I looked down from the turret, smirked, gave them a look that would rival Dirty Harry, and said in a low and confident voice, "Let's do this." They all nodded back without saying a word. I could see the discipline in their eyes. It was more than just motivation. Over time, their training and preparation turned their motivation into sheer discipline. It was time to get to work. It's amazing how stress can bring out the best or the worst in you.

Elements of our battalion raided the village just as the sun was creeping over the peaks of the Chāgai Hills. Taliban forces in Bahram Cha were just waking up when we stormed their streets with LAVs, MATVs, and a force of Marines that was typical of our kind—overpowering. Throughout that day, we detained twenty-one suspects for questioning, identified two enemy command and control nodes, neutralized several enemy combatants, and seized more than 4,400 kilograms of opium, 1,750 kilograms of ammonium nitrate, and seventy IED components. It was a good day. Our presence severely restricted Taliban movement and forced the enemy to shift its trafficking routes farther west and east into the desert.

However, what made it an even better day was that even though we planned on several Marine Corps and coalition casualties, the only injuries to friendly forces were a twisted ankle and one Afghani Army gunshot wound to the hip. For me, the ultimate measure of success was bringing every one of my Marines home that day. Success had never tasted sweeter. Like I said, it was a good day!

Success was ours. However, there is a saying that applies to much, if not all, of life: "This too shall pass." A few days later, we returned to base, and it wasn't to a roaring crowd. There was no bonus for doing a good job, no standing ovations, and no increased social media followers. The victory was celebrated the best way we knew how—with a round of cigars around a fire pit while drawing up plans for how we would pack up and head home. There was still so much to do, and we had to create a plan and execute that plan flawlessly. The victory was won, but there was still work to be done.

Success isn't a one-time thing, and at the same time, it's not a guarantee. I hope success is something every team will experience often, but my deeper hope is that we never become satisfied with our success and that we use what we learn to replicate success. I'm not saying that we can't celebrate and honor our victories; we *must* celebrate and honor our teams as they succeed, but there is always something else to go after. There is always someone looking to be better than you. There will always be another storm to face. The greats like Kobe Bryant, Michael Jordan, Mike Tyson, and Tom Brady were vicious in their pursuit of repeated success. Their work ethic, drive, and inability to be satisfied with one victory are what made them and their teams great.

You will hear me say this throughout this book. Leadership is one of the hardest things a person can sign up for. Hell, I don't know why anyone would want to lead. Isn't it so much easier to sit back and be told what to do and how to do it? Sure, it is. However, for those who have chosen… No… If we are blessed with the honor and privilege of leading, we must understand how success can cause us to slip. Yes, we have to celebrate it, but there is a ton we must learn from success as well. Here are a few ways we can ensure that our success doesn't go to waste.

ACTION STEPS

Celebrate the win with your team.

One of the greatest basketball coaches of all time Glenn Anton Rivers, better known to the rest of us as Doc Rivers, led his herd through this storm better than most, and it wasn't because he was a singularly gifted coach. He was, but that wasn't the special sauce to his success. Instead of focusing on his all-star players and building his playbook around them, he took an old African proverb called Ubuntu. The core concept of Ubuntu is the phrase, "I am because we are." The concept of Ubuntu is that you succeed together as a team.

Yes, you succeeded. No, you didn't succeed by yourself. There are so many people involved in each success. Mike Tyson threw the punches, but his trainers made him jump rope. Tom Brady threw the football, but his receivers had to catch the ball. When we succeed, we must celebrate and give credit where credit is due. Often, leaders can get caught in a very selfish mindset, believing that they are responsible for the team's success. We absolutely play a part in the success, but the people around us truly complete the equation.

Spend time detailing your after-action report.

This is a best practice for both failure and success. Creating an after-action report from any event, sales cycle, briefing, presentation, grant submission, or anything else will give you a chance to pull out the "whys" of your success. Take inventory of pivotal moments in the process that had an impact and see if you can make them repeatable. Here's an outline of an after-action report to use with your teams and adapt as you see fit. It's quite simple.

1) What went well and why?

2) What didn't go well and why?

3) What should be done differently next time and why?

After that final operation, we had to understand that there was always another job to do, and we had to succeed. Success is only a one-time thing if you stop progressing—if you stop learning. No matter what industry you are in or how many successes you have, there is always room for improvement. This after-action report will help you identify the opportunities for improvement because there is always something that could have gone better, and by collecting this information, you will be better prepared to thrive in the next leadership storm.

Assess the strengths and opportunities of your team.

This step of the success process will equip you for your next challenge. Throughout the process of succeeding, you have undoubtedly discovered a few hidden talents on your team that you didn't know were there. "Wow, John really stepped up his communication with the team," or "Traci took charge and got things done." As you unpack what happened, take note of these nuggets of rock stardom, and as you begin the next task, mission, or challenge, lean on the Johns and Tracis of the team to help achieve that sweet and satisfying feeling that comes with succeeding.

Also, identify opportunities for growth. "Man, John communicated really well, but he was moving a bit too fast and was unorganized at times," or "Traci led really well but was a bit of a bulldozer to her peers." Take this information and create plans for sharpening the skills that need to be sharpened by giving your team positive and constructive feedback. Feedback is *gold*, but to be useful, we must be willing to accept it. Yes, the leadership team as well. Once the feedback is collected, given, and accepted, create plans for improving and learning. In business, if you aren't growing (both financially and personally), you are dying.

Through celebrating, creating after-action reports, and identifying strengths and opportunities through generating feedback, you will find that you and your team are stronger and far better prepared for the next challenge or storm. Success is what we all aim for, but there are always different levels of success. Within success, there are failures and things that could have gone better. We can't dwell on these failures, but we can learn from them and strengthen the herd as we prepare for what's next. Success should not lead to complacency or laziness but should be a platform for further learning and growth. As leaders, we must continuously improve ourselves and our teams to best prepare for the storms to come.

Going back to Afghanistan, one of the most effective companies during that operation was led by my good friend, John Bitonti. He was a battle-hardened Marine Corps captain and hand-selected by our battalion commander to lead a company in one of the most effective units in the Marine Corps. Throughout the deployment, John led his company on some of the most important missions our battalion was tasked with. John was also Jacob Leicht's company commander and recently told me a short but powerful story, one that I never knew, and it filled my soul with gratitude.

On the night that Jacob was killed, the rest of his platoon returned to base to debrief and take a breath after what happened. They got some chow, showered, and went back to their tent to figure out what was next. As John walked into their tent, he noticed the Marines were all spread out. Some were in the corner, not saying a word. Some were in the back of the tent, fuming with anger and kicking and throwing anything they could reach. John says that the tension in that tent was so heavy you could feel it as soon as you walked in. John looked around, took inventory of the emotions in the tent, and said, "Gents, this sucks. The only thing I know how to do during times like this is pray. I'm not ordering any of you to join in, but I will start. Join in if you want to." Every Marine in the tent walked over to John, and arm and arm, they prayed. John said that as they prayed, the tension in the room disappeared.

That's the kind of leader John is and the kind of leader I long to be. His leadership scars were well-earned, and his storms began years before we ever stepped foot in Afghanistan. John has plowed through some of the toughest storms imaginable. The toughest was in Fallujah, Iraq, in 2004 during Operation Phantom Fury. John's story is the focus of the next storm we will go through together. Buckle up, folks. This storm would drive most of us to our knees.

Afghanistan Pictures

4

THE STORM OF LEADING
FROM THE FRONT (PART 1):
OPERATION PHANTOM FURY

A heavy winter storm's adverse conditions can kill the strongest buffalo. These storms can come out of nowhere and are almost always stronger than predicted. Frigid temperatures, blowing snow, and treacherous terrain are only a small portion of what can kill off an entire herd. I haven't even talked about the massive number of predators out there just waiting for one of the herd to split off on its own, making it a prime target for a winter meal. Nevertheless, the head buffalo charges on into the storm, leading the herd into an environment that could absolutely kill them.

In 2004, the city of Fallujah, Iraq, was overtaken by a storm like this. The city was in shambles; people were being tortured and killed, and US forces had lost control of the city. The roughly nine-year Operation Iraqi Freedom conflict was barely a year old. The fighting was getting more and more intense by the day, and more and more US military lives were being lost. Then, in March 2004, a string of events initiated a chain reaction that would define a generation of Marines. The first was the ambush and brutal murder of four US government contractors: Wesley Batalona, Scott Helvenston, Jerry Zovko, and Michael Teague. The second was the hanging of their bodies from a bridge in the center of town, and the third was displaying this brutality across media outlets worldwide. To say that this really pissed us off is a dramatic understatement.

In April 2004, because of the events that had unfolded in the months prior, the Marine Corps kicked off Operation Vigilant Resolve in an attempt to take back control of Fallujah from the insurgents that haunted the city. After only a few weeks, the operation ended with a promise from the Iraqi people stating they would keep the insurgents out of the city. Looking back, this was something we should have known was an impossibility.

Over the next few months, the insurgent population began to grow. Members of al-Qaida in Iraq (AQI), the Islamic Army of Iraq (IAI), Ansar al-Suna, and a slew of other insurgent groups began to stage themselves within the city. It's unclear how many fighters were in the city, but some estimate up to five thousand made up of what intelligence reports have determined to be Saudi, Chechen, Libyan, Filipino, and Syrian combatants, as well as Iraqis. They were gearing up for the inevitable offensive with US forces. The enemy was ready, the civilians were warned, and in November of 2004, the US Military launched Operation Phantom Fury.

Phantom Fury, also known as the second battle of Fallujah, will go down in Marine Corps and military history as the most intense and violent six weeks in nearly nine years of Operation Iraqi Freedom (OIF), and some say it was the heaviest engagement in urban combat since the Vietnam War. Prior to beginning the operation, US and coalition forces had established checkpoints around the city to allow civilians to flee to safety and to prevent insurgents from leaving. Intelligence was collected and analyzed to create a grid system for the city. Fallujah was to be strategically and systematically cleared of insurgents block by block. The Marines, including a small platoon of heroes led by First Lieutenant John Bitonti, were given one of Fallujah's most deadly and kinetic blocks.

While I never had the honor of serving with John in Iraq, as I mentioned earlier, John and I served together in Afghanistan. We were able to push through some of the most difficult storms imaginable. John is a true warrior and a Marine I would trust with all my children's lives. He is a man of integrity, grit, focus, faith, kindness, and so much more. His leadership is directly correlated with saving lives because of his deep concern for mission accomplishment, doing things the right way, and taking care of his people. This is John's account of Operation Phantom Fury and is a true example of how we can lead from the front with the utmost integrity, valor, and courage. It's also an example of how we can come out on the other side of this storm better leaders and better prepared for the next storm that will inevitably come over the horizon. John leads from the front, never ordering anyone to do something he isn't 100 percent willing to do himself. This is John's story, told in his words. In life, our stories carry us through storms—through amazing times and some of the worst times imaginable. They are ours and are ours to tell, and this is John's.

John was a California kid who grew up knowing he would become a Marine Corps officer. His dad was a Marine, so in their house, they didn't play soldier; they played Marine, and they all worked together serving food at their family restaurant. A tough kid, John often ran with the party crowd but was focused on family and football, playing all four years of high school. Being the youngest on the team meant he had to work twice as hard, and it paid off his senior year, as John was one of the best players on the field.

After high school, John continued his pursuit of Marine Corps greatness, but school was tough. He was a Marine Corps reservist and worked over forty hours a week on campus and at the family restaurant. He struggled to keep up academically, bouncing around from three different local colleges and taking some time off. These days were hard for John, but he never took his eyes off the prize. He was determined to graduate and become the man he always wanted to be, and after a few years of grinding, he graduated. Next stop, Marine Corps Officer Candidate School (OCS)!

Marine Corps OCS is no walk in the park. It's considered by many to be the most challenging officer candidate school in the United States Military, but John wasn't fazed by it. He'd wanted this since he was a kid and could shake off the screaming and bed flipping. Nothing was stopping him from becoming the best damn infantry officer in the Marine Corps. Following OCS is The Basic School (TBS), where John learned all the things he needed to know about the Marine Corps. He learned when and where to salute, Marine Corps history, tidbits of war strategy, and other basics that Marine Corps officers need to know before they head off to their specific Military Occupational Specialty (MOS) school, which for John was the Infantry Officers Course (IOC), a fifteen-week program meant to train each infantry officer on every weapon system the Marine Corps had and to equip them with the leadership tools they would need to lead in an infantry battalion.

I share this part of John's story because it highlights where John came from and sets the stage for Fallujah, 2004. Marine Corps officers go through some of the most stringent and intense training our military can conjure. They spend over a year tired, wet, and hungry, but that's all part of the process of making Marine Corps officers. These men and women are responsible for accomplishing our country's most critical missions as well as leading enlisted Marines through some of the most dangerous landscapes imaginable. John was a steely-eyed, well-trained Marine Corps officer who would eventually use every bit of training he received. For him, it was a dream come true.

After all the training that molded John into the Marine he always knew he would be, it was time to get after it. As a brand-new second lieutenant, he was sent to his first duty station, 3rd Light Armored Recon Battalion (LAR), in beautiful 29 Palms, California, and then quickly shipped off to Kuwait for the invasion of Iraq in 2002. While the Iraq invasion story could be a whole book in and of itself, our story begins when John returns home. Upon returning from the invasion in 2003, John became the company executive officer as a newly promoted first lieutenant.

Shortly after settling into his new role, John was given a few choices about his future. He passed up the opportunity to go to a B-Billet with his peers and head out to recruiting duty, drill instructor duty, and several other mostly non-combat-related positions. Instead, he had the option to stay on for another deployment to Iraq or take charge of a platoon being attached to the 31st Marine Expeditionary Unit (MEU) launching from Okinawa, Japan. For some context, a MEU is a mobile response unit that usually stays at sea but is launched in case of emerging global instability—kind of a "break glass in case of emergency" unit.

John was faced with a choice, and given that he was one of the more senior lieutenants in the battalion, he had to choose his own adventure. His current company would join the rest of his unit already in Iraq, so he had to make a quick decision. John walked into his boss' office and said, "Sir, I'll do whatever you need me to do, but I know there are some new lieutenants whose careers would really benefit from an Iraq deployment. My thoughts are to give one of the newer lieutenants a chance. I got the T-shirt. I'm good. I'll jump on the MEU." John chose to join the MEU in Okinawa, Japan, to give up his spot on another Iraq deployment to another

Marine—or so he thought. John was a hot commodity within the battalion, and the company commander wanted him to remain the company executive officer in Iraq; however, being the leader he was, he chose to let someone else step in and build their career.

The MEU deployment was only a few months away, and John was sitting in 29 Palms without a Marine to call his own. "I'm like four months away from deploying to Okinawa, and I don't have a platoon; I don't know where we are going— nothing." So, in response to John's consistent inquiry as to what the hell he was going to do, the 3rd LAR commander's office sent a message to the companies to pony up Marines to fill John's platoon. This is not the best process by which to receive stellar, hard-charging Marines into your platoon. Whenever a message like this goes out, leaders take inventory of their very best and guard those Marines with their lives. There is no way the company will give up their best Marines to a MEU platoon months before an Iraq deployment. In the end, 3rd LAR did not even provide a full platoon—no staff-level non-commissioned officer, three junior corporals, and four non-infantry Marines to serve as infantry scouts.

As a result, John received a ragtag group of Marines—some just pulled the short straw; others were ready to get out of the Marine Corps; some were out of shape, and most just didn't want to be there. The shining star in all this was a senior staff sergeant who was as salty as they come. A twenty-year staff sergeant who didn't look the part was John's right-hand man in putting this group together and shaping them into the unit they would eventually become. He was old but experienced. John described him as a guy who "didn't take crap from any-one but cared deeply about his Marines." You get the picture. So, after some initial training, John and his new platoon were shipped off to Okinawa to join up with the MEU.

The thought process behind the 31st MEU deployment was that this group of Marines was going on a cruise somewhere in the Indo-Pacific. They would move from port to port, train with their weapon systems, lift weights, and eat the Navy's food. The last time the 31st MEU went into combat was the Vietnam War, but boy was that all about to change. John and his newly formed platoon were about to make Marine Corps history. In fact, John found out there was a chance the 31st MEU might end up in a combat zone, but the response from his battalion leadership was, "Don't worry, the 31st MEU never goes anywhere."

A few months after arriving in Okinawa, John was called at midnight to come into the Battalion Landing Team commander's office. The Battalion Landing Team (BLT) is the unit on the MEU that gets called into combat if necessary. Having no idea what was going on and eight hours into one of the certification exercises for an Indo-Pacific tour, he wiped the crust from his eyes and stumbled into the office. LtCol Ramos said to John, "Pack your stuff and get your guys ready. You're headed to Kuwait." John responded, "Whoa, okay. I'll get the guys ready. Iraq?" LtCol Ramos responded, "We don't know if it is Iraq or Afghanistan, but one of them for sure."

In less than forty-eight hours, the unit was trained, packed, and headed to Kuwait and eventually staged for their push into the city of Fallujah. His platoon would be attached to a larger battalion already staged and waiting for him to get there. They spent two weeks in Kuwait before heading north toward the city. This was the only cohesive and comprehensive training his platoon had conducted since coming together.

As the Battalion Landing Team arrived at Camp Fallujah, they were greeted by a metaphorical NO VACANCY sign flashing as they rolled in. "We are completely packed, and we had no idea you guys were coming," the camp commander forcefully stated. The commander of John's unit simply replied,

"We're a battalion of Marines. We're huge. Where are we supposed to go?" After a few minutes of back and forth, the camp commander pointed to an area on the base where they could set up tents and have reinforced walls for their head-quarters area. This area of the camp was known as the Iranian Training Center, a former Iranian training camp with a few hard structures and room for tents.

As the battalion drove down the road to their new home, the Explosive Ordinance Disposal (EOD) contractors were detonating mortar and artillery rounds that hit the ground but never detonated on the road in front of them. "We were literally driving by exploding ordinance on our way to set up our camp in the ITC. To these guys, it's totally normal. Like 'just another Wednesday' kind of stuff." The old Iranian training camp was surrounded by open fields, allowing them to see directly into the city from across the camp. It was a dangerous place to call home, even for Camp Fallujah. As they were waiting to set up camp, before they set up their first tent, they were hit with an accurate mortar attack, causing the first casualty of Operation Phantom Fury 2. They had been at Camp Fallujah for less than twenty-four hours.

In October 2004, after they were set up as best they could, they were tasked with maintaining and clearing the main sup-ply routes leading to and past the cities of Fallujah and Ramadi. Clearing meant they were driving targets. Their job was to drive down the main supply roads leading to Fallujah, clearing the path so resources could get to and from the camp. A few hours into the first day of actual operations, John's company and another platoon ran over an IED, disabling one of their vehicles immediately. In the first week, the BLT lost eleven Marines. One to a vehicle rollover and ten to a vehicle-borne improvised explosive device (VBIED) that detonated right next to their seven-ton truck, killing every Marine inside. "This was the kind of environment we were in. The enemy knew we were there and knew where we were going. It was hot. We were in contact constantly."

After a short time of route-security operations, they were given the word that they were headed into the city of Fallujah to clear the town of insurgents. At first, John was under the impression that they were going to sit on the perimeter of the city and provide overwatch, but that was never the plan. John had a solid reputation, and his platoon was being built into the plan to take back the city. It is a little-known fact that LAR was physically fighting, house-to-house, during Operation Phantom Fury. LAR is a mounted organization, meaning they are in vehicles—LAVs, to be exact. Urban, door-to-door warfare isn't a part of their training regiment, so John had to adapt, once again, to having to learn something new, lead from the front, and teach his Marines how to do the impossible in an impossible situation.

The uncertainty and changes kept coming. John's platoon was reassigned, yet again, to another battalion to support the initial attack on Fallujah. However, that didn't faze him at this point. He jumped into action, planning for whatever they would be ordered to do. He was used to dealing with impossible odds and the uncertainty of absolutely everything around him. Over the last five months, his Marines had grown to love and trust him with their lives, so as John was dealing with the big-picture strategy with the senior leaders, his Marines were preparing themselves for door-to-door combat. John trusted his Marines to run drills, provide tweaks, and train to the standard he set. This group of Marines that were thrown together on a whim were gelling into a world-class fighting force that would become like family. They prepared, equipped, and got themselves ready for something they had never done before.

On November 8, 2004, John's platoon moved into position on the city's north side and prepared to move in. They staged one hundred meters on the northern edge of the city and waited for the call, and as they waited, they watched. They could see IEDs hanging from the bridges they were supposed to cross to get into the city. "They were literally blowing in the wind," John described. On November 9, surrounded by Marines from other battalions already engaged, John and his Marines readied themselves for their assault. Operation Phantom Fury was about to begin.

On the night of the 9th, staged just outside the city, the only light that John's platoon could see was from the absolute chaos happening within the city. "The sky was on fire," John recalled. Rockets, tracer rounds, explosions, and voices shouting orders drowned out any signs of everyday city life. Like a caged pit bull being taunted with a steak dinner, John's Marines awaited their orders to begin to move, but as they waited, they began to see movement in the buildings in front of them. "Sir, we got movement from east to west in the buildings about fifty meters in front of us. We see people moving through the windows of the buildings, Sir."

John hopped on the radio to report what they were seeing to senior leadership. "We have a group of unidentified individuals moving between and within the buildings in front of us. They are definitely organizing for something."

One of the problems at the time was that John's platoon wasn't equipped with high-tech night vision equipment, and there were friendly forces (other Marines) operating in the area. "Were these guys friendly or not? We really couldn't tell."

For context, Marines operating in the area were *supposed* to have an infrared blinking light on the back of their helmets, and they were to be turned on during nighttime operations. These lights can only be seen through other friendly forces' night vision equipment to identify them as friendly forces. This group had no such indicator, so John was given the green light to make a decision. The response came back over the radio, "Take the shot if you need to take the shot." It's an ambiguous order if I've ever heard one.

John and his Marines continued to watch the movement within and around the buildings, waiting for positive identification of some kind of enemy activity, but John had a horrible feeling. Relying on his instincts and outstanding leadership ability, he gave his gunner the green light to engage the dirt and the lower bottom portion of the building but nothing else. His gunner engaged the base of the building and the dirt with three shots. *Boom! Boom! Boom!* Dust and debris flew into the air with the impact of the 25mm rounds on the base of the building. At the sound and feel of the effects, the unknown group froze, and after a few short seconds, which felt like hours, John watched them unfreeze, reach toward the back of their heads, and turn on the friendly blinking infrared light. Had it not been for John's gut feeling and his ability to discern an extremely difficult situation, John's platoon would have annihilated all the Marines in those buildings.

The decision-making process that John went through during that time was self-described as "energy and patience." It takes energy and patience to make decisions. It's easy to make a quick decision, and yes, sometimes quick decisions need to be made, especially in combat. However, the energy it takes to create a plan that thoroughly addresses a problem and not act on it immediately saved the lives of a dozen Marines that night. John had the energy required to decide and the patience to simply see what happened.

As John's platoon was still waiting to go into the city and after a few hours of watching, staging, and recovering from what would have been an international incident, the clock turned to midnight, November 10, 2004—the Marine Corps' birthday. The Marine Corps was founded in a bar in Philadelphia 229 years earlier. In 1775, the Marine Corps was formed and given its legitimacy as what would one day become the world's most indomitable fighting force. It's a long-held Marine Corps tradition that Marines get together no matter where they are to share a piece of cake, read the birthday message from the current commandant, share a pint, and read a message from the 13th Commandant of the Marine Corps Lieutenant General John a Lejeune. John wouldn't let this year be any different. John and his platoon were becoming a part of Marine Corps history. But first, cake.

Just after midnight, John sent a radio message to all his Marines that he would be coming to each vehicle to provide updated orders. The Marines were tired, hungry, anxious, and ready to fight, but that wouldn't halt tradition. John stepped out of his vehicle, dusty and still shaken from what happened just hours earlier, and proceeded to go from vehicle to vehicle to vehicle, stopping at each one to shake the hands of his Marines, wish them a happy birthday, and read both commandant's birthday messages. Before leaving each vehicle to go to the next, he reminded the Marines why they were there. He reminded them that they had a job to do and that they were minutes away from doing just that. This simple act had an immeasurable impact on his Marines. They were ecstatic, re-motivated, cheering, and grunting as John moved on to the next vehicle. "Get your gear together because we enter the city at 0600." He inspired his Marines to perform in the most difficult environments to ever exist, all in the name of leadership.

At 0600, John and his platoon were given the order to assault, secure, and hold the government center operationally named "Division Objective One." This wouldn't be easy. Surrounding the government center were several tall buildings, a mosque, and an unknown number of insurgents just waiting for a chance to fight. The enemy had the high ground, and the Marines would have to fight from the ground up.

John's platoon started moving toward their objective in the early morning hours of November 10. As they moved toward their objective, it was eerily quiet. It was dead quiet besides the sounds of dogs barking and their vehicles. They moved through the main roads of the city slowly and deliberately, watching for IEDs buried in dead animals or abandoned vehicles. Their route was covered with vehicles and buildings that were still on fire from the fighting the night before, and the carnage of war was all around them. As they moved toward their objective, John's Marines were on edge but baffled by the stillness of it all. The explosions and small arms fire from the night before were non-existent at this point, and it was dangerously quiet. As they approached their objective, the sun began to crest over the tops of the buildings, warming the Marines' faces, and then, as if it were timed with the sunrise, all hell broke loose.

Division Objective One was an open area in the shape of a square built perfectly for an enemy ambush. On the forward edge of the square was a basketball court, a schoolhouse, and a few other government buildings. As John and his Marines moved into fighting positions, they were inundated with sniper fire, rocket-propelled grenades, and machine gun fire simultaneously. It was all they could do to find a defensible position on the square for their four not-so-maneuverable vehicles. They had to get into a position to fight back.

After finally putting all his vehicles into position, the fighting heated up. John and his Marines were engaging with every weapon they had. John was hanging out of the top of his vehicle, giving orders on the ground, and his Marines were firing their weapons at the surrounding buildings. It was total but controlled chaos. John was shooting and giving orders from his vehicle when he heard the firing of an RPG from the Mosque across the street, and it was heading straight for him. As if in slow motion, the round flew by his head, missing by only a few feet, but the rocket hit and went through the wall behind his vehicle. While it was a close call for John, one of his vehicles and the Marines within were on the other side of that wall and were not so lucky. The round hit the vehicle behind the wall, causing the first casualty from John's platoon. One of his Marines, the driver, sustained severe shrapnel wounds to the left side of his body and had to be medevac'd immediately. He would survive but would have to be airlifted out of Iraq, leaving John's platoon one Marine down.

They were now being shot at from every angle, and after a few hours of fighting, John had to get his Marines to a place where they could rest for a bit and refill on fuel and ammunition. They pulled back from the forward edge and into more covered positions so John could check in with his leaders, who were firmly established in one of the main buildings on *Division Objective One*. John and a few of his Marines dismounted, including Lance Corporal Magaoay. They dismounted and made their way to a stairwell on the backside of a secured building. The firefight on the other side of the building had slowed down, but they needed to check in and debrief with leadership. As they walked up the stairs to get to where the other Marines were, the impact and reality of what was happening around them hit them in the worst way. A Marine Corps officer was being carried down the stairs on a stretcher—he was dead. He had been killed in the firefight that they were just in. This Marine was the first officer killed in Fallujah, and that was the moment it became real for everyone. For the enlisted Marines, an officer is invincible; they can't die. The hard reality changed the tone of the deployment at that very moment. Their faces turned from young enlisted men to Marines who were faced with the reality that death is a real possibility. Not only that, but it can happen to any one of them at any time.

After John checked in with his company commander, and he and his Marines started back down the stairs to their vehicles, the firefight had picked back up again—this time with sniper fire. They departed the mayor's building and had to cross a large open driveway over to the police station, where you could hear rounds zipping by and explosions continuing all around. Once again, John's leadership intuition kicked in. As the first two scouts went to the far side of the driveway, John said, "Magaoay, you guys cover me. Basilio and I will cross over and cover you from the other side. On three, we're going to take off. There is sniper fire from the east and south. Make sure you cover us. Basilio, you follow me."

John took a few deep breaths as his Marines got into firing positions to cover his movement to the other side. "1… 2… 3… Go!" John took off across the driveway but got no more than two steps into the sprint when he tripped over the curb, flew through the air, and jammed his shin into the concrete curb—hard. John hit the pavement so hard that he couldn't move; the air was immediately expelled from his entire body. He was wearing fifty pounds of gear and was laying on the bridge, motionless, and his Marines thought the worst. *The Sir has been shot.* "Sir, Sir! Are you okay?"

With a slight raise of his left hand and with a painful, breathless mumble, he said, "I'm fine. I'm good."

His Marines were relieved but holding back bursts of laughter at John's expense. After a moment of recovery, John, Basilio, and the rest of his Marines made it safely across the road into the cover of a police station. He turned to them with a stone-cold look on his face. The one that your father gives you when you break something, but your mom is in the room. His Marines could barely hold their composure, holding their breath, bodies jostling from internal laughter. They wanted nothing more than to crack up and give John a hard time, but he was the boss, so they technically couldn't.

John took a breath and said to them quietly, "Okay. You have ten seconds. Go."

The Marines lost their minds with laughter and trash talk for ten seconds. After that glorious ten seconds, John responded in a hilariously serious tone, "Okay, zip it. We don't ever talk about this again. If anyone ever asks about it, I was saving Basilio's life." John gave them a sense of humanity for ten seconds at his expense.

After John and his Marines got back to the vehicles and took a short break, John was set loose to occupy fighting positions on the forward edge of *Division Objective One*. They were back in the fight. The intense fighting from November 10 lasted twenty-seven hours, bleeding well into the afternoon of November 11.

The rest of the city was still under insurgents' control, but John and his Marines were well on their way to securing their objective. After almost two straight days of fighting, John and his Marines successfully secured *Division Objective One*. They headed back to a fuel ammunition resupply point just outside the city to rest, refuel, and refit.

November 11 is Veterans Day, but it also happens to be John's birthday. John told his Marines to clean their weapons, grab ammunition, rest up, and eat. They were going to be back at it sooner than they would realize. After a few hours out of the city, John's Marines took the opportunity to celebrate their fearless leader. As John was preparing the platoon to return and talking with some other leaders, his Marines showed up with an MRE pound cake, a lit cigarette for a candle, and a can of Red Bull.

"Happy Birthday, Sir!" LCpl Magaoay shouted.

John's response was simple, "Where the hell did you guys get a Red Bull?"

5

THE STORM OF LEADING
FROM THE FRONT (PART 2):
OPERATION PHANTOM FURY,
A NEW MISSION

Their rest at the fuel ammunition resupply point would be short-lived as they were soon headed back into the city with a new set of orders. *Division Objective One* was secure, and it was time for John's Marines, attached to their parent battalion, to move on to something else—house-clearing operations in the heart of Fallujah. John and his Marines were to use their vehicles and scouts to clear the city's most dangerous streets. They knew they would eventually be tasked with the larger mission of taking back the city, and now, it was happening. They made their way toward their new objective rested, motivated, and unsure of what would happen.

John received orders to take up positions along the main supply routes through Fallujah to secure resupply operations, and John set his vehicles in place along the route with other traditional Marine Corps infantry platoons, getting ready to clear the city blocks ahead of them. Just before they were given the order to move forward to provide support, a vehicle from another platoon pulled up beside them with two casualties, one of them being Staff Sergeant Holder, an old friend of Johns. Staff Sergeant Holder was killed immediately by machine gun fire. John and SSgt Holder were together in Okinawa, where John was putting together his platoon until Holder was promoted from sergeant to staff sergeant. Holder even selected John to pin on his rank when he was promoted, which was a huge honor. Now, SSgt Holder was gone, but the fighting never stopped. With a broken heart, John said to his Marines, "Holder is here with us in spirit, but we still have a job to do."

Over the next several days, John and his Marines went house to house, clearing the streets of Fallujah of enemy fighters and IEDs. Day patrols were filled with hours of fighting, and night raids were mixed in with sleep rotations. As he and his Marines cleared the neighborhoods, they began to notice something. The United States Military had been in these houses and had been, shall we say, less than respectful of the homes in which they were occupying. The houses were trashed, and hygiene took a backseat to convenience. It was as if they didn't understand that these were people's homes that they would someday return to. John recalled, "Imagine being forced to leave your home because of war. You had to leave unexpectedly and without any of your belongings. Pictures, letters, personal belongings, and furniture all had to be left behind. In what state would you want your home to be in when you returned?"

John saw what was happening and gave his Marines strict orders to take good care of the homes they occupied, even if only for a short while, putting dignity and respect above vengeance and contempt. His Marines would be different, never destroying anything that didn't need to be destroyed. "You aren't just responsible for the now, but you are responsible for what happens later." He recalled, "You need to know that you conducted yourself with the utmost integrity, discipline, and respect. Don't leave anything on the table that you are going to regret. We will live on values and not violence." They would move from house to house, day after day, fighting an enemy that was often unseen. John's vehicles and Marines were taking a beating, but nevertheless, they pushed through the city.

The standard operating procedure for John's platoon was simple. Marine Corps scouts would set in overwatch of the vehicles and infantry platoons, and they'd clear houses after the vehicles had passed. Ahead of the vehicles were fireteams meant to do the initial clearing of the area, making sure it was safe for the vehicle and the rest of the scouts to move forward. Heavy fighting from house to house was causing significant casualties for his Marines and those from other platoons. Repeatedly, John's vehicles were loaded up with injured Marines to be taken out of the fight, but as quickly as they could be turned over to the medics, John was back in the fight.

With the platoon taking on heavy casualties, John took over a fire station as their mini headquarters. This was a fortified spot where they could plan, rest, and reload ammunition. However, the afternoon of the 29th would be one that John would call one of the hardest days of his life. Lance Corporal Magaoay, one of the Marines from John's earlier face plant, was close to John, naming himself the "official bodyguard of the Sir (John)." Magaoay went everywhere with John to make sure John was protected. That afternoon, Magaoay and three other Marines left the safety of the fire station to investigate and clear a building across the street. John had just returned from receiving his orders to continue "search and attacks" and was beginning to plan for the next mission when suddenly, he heard a machine gun fire and grenades go off across the street.

No more than thirty seconds later, one of the Marines came into the station holding his stomach. He and another one of the three were both shot in the stomach as they cleared the house across the street. John ran over to them, and they said, "Magaoay is still in the house."

John grabbed the Marines who were in the fire station and said, "Let's go get him."

The homes in Fallujah were reinforced with bars on the windows and a heavy door; this one was no different. John and his Marines were immediately met with machine gun fire from the windows of the building. Not knowing where Magaoay was or whether he was alive or not, John and his Marines had to be careful to return fire. They strategically returned fire and engaged in a forty-five-minute firefight from outside the building, and as the Marines moved closer to the building, they began to take casualties. John knew that Magaoay was likely dead inside, and he was filled with rage. He charged toward the front door in a violent effort to retrieve Magaoay's body, but as he got to the front door, one of his Marines, last name Sanchez, slammed him against the wall. "Sir, you don't go in first! We need you alive. We got this." His Marines finally breached the house, cleared the house of the remaining insurgents, and pulled Magaoay's body out. John's fears were realized: Magaoay had been killed.

As John's Marines carried Magaoay's body back to the fire station and got him prepared for evacuation, John continued to fight the insurgents left in the house. With Magoay secured, John pulled the Marines away from the house, cordoned it off, took four scouts to the roof of the fire station, and fired four simultaneous thermogenic rockets into the first and second stories, devastating the building and everything inside of it. This part of the fight was over, but now, we were dealing with the aftermath.

The Marines stripped Magoay's protective equipment and uniform to deliver whatever first aid they could, but it was too late. The Marines were devastated, and so was John. John thought to himself, *The boys can't see this.* Magaoay was in a pool of blood. John started screaming at his platoon sergeant, Sgt Garcia, to get him rags, bottles of water, and trash bags so he could clean up the scene. He threw Magaoay's bloody uniform into the trash bags and violently began cleaning up the blood with the dirty rags he'd been given. He didn't want his Marines to see what was happening. He had to keep them in the fight. Hell, *he* had to get back in the fight.

After Magaoay's death, John was shattered. However, he knew he had to continue—not for himself, but for his Marines, for Magaoay, and for every other Marine, soldier, and sailor who had been killed during the previous months.

The night turned to morning, Magaoay was taken out of Fallujah and sent home, and after a few more weeks of intense fighting, on Christmas Eve of 2004, Operation Phantom Fury came to an end. The City of Fallujah was mostly cleared of the enemy force that once held it hostage—at least for the time being.

Over the next several months, John and his Marines would travel across Iraq doing much of the same—mission after mission, casualty after casualty, accomplishment after accomplishment. He led his Marines for the next eight months and beyond through the most difficult storms a human can go through, never wavering on discipline, caring for his Marines, and leading from the front. John is a true hero and leader of leaders. He is a man who exemplifies what it means to take care of your people. I could go on forever about his heroics and accomplishments, but let's start to dissect and learn from the storm that was Operation Phantom Fury.

ACTION STEPS

Leading from the front is one of the best but most difficult ways to lead, but it requires quick decision-making under pressure. Leading this way puts you in vulnerable positions, opens you up to criticism, and increases the stakes. John led his Marines from the front in so many ways, but the theme of his style is leading by example, integrity above all else, and never telling your people to do anything you aren't willing to do yourself. Here's how you can apply this lesson in your leadership journey.

Lead by Example

Throughout John's story, he continuously leads by example, even when he isn't supposed to. Many times, his Marines had to hold him back from running into a building full of insurgents to save or retrieve one of his Marines. So, how do we lead by example with our teams, organizations, and even our community? Like the buffalo, we need to take the lead and charge through the storm, whatever storm that may be, regardless of the outcome. Leaders take ownership of the situation because the herd needs to be led through the storm. Embracing this ownership is far more about mindset than skillset. Leaders have to want ownership.

A great example of this was the late Kobe Bryant, "The Black Mamba." Kobe always wanted the ball when the game was on the line. He will go down in history as one of the greatest basketball players of all time, but it isn't just his amazing skills on the court that people will remember. Kobe was the best because he wanted to be the best, and he wanted it more than anyone else on the court. His work ethic is what made him the best. He would be at practice before, longer, and later than anyone else on the team. He would be in the weight room when others were at the nightclubs and running laps when others were asleep. He didn't want to be the next Michael Jordan. He wanted to be the only Kobe Bryant.

However, not everyone loved Kobe. In fact, other all-stars didn't like him or his attitude, but that didn't faze him or his work ethic.

There's a big misconception where people thinking winning or success comes from everybody putting their arms
around each other and singing kumbaya and patting them
on the back when they mess up, and that's just not reality.
If you are going to be a leader, you are not going to please
everybody. You have to hold people accountable. Even if
you have that moment of being uncomfortable.

–Kobe Bryant

Kobe took ownership of his greatness. He knew what he
wanted his outcome to be and owned the process of making
that outcome a reality. He owned his success and took responsibility for his failures, but he never let anyone get in the way of
his success, and the outcome was that his teammates followed
him through the storms of professional sports. The world of
sports can be brutal. One second, you are praised by reports
and fans alike and the next, you are hated by the world. As a
leader, Kobe never let the media or outside influences phase
his launch to greatness. He owned every shot he took and
worked hard so his team would give him the opportunity to
take the most important ones.

But what's the difference between taking responsibility
and taking ownership? When a leader says, "I take full responsibility for what happened," it is often after something bad
has happened. I can't imagine a good leader coming into a
situation after some measure of success and saying, "I take
full responsibility for what happened." These types of leaders
usually aren't in their positions for long. We use the *responsibility* term after the fact. Yes, it's also used preemptively, but
most of the time, we take responsibility for something that's
already happened.

Taking ownership is something that leaders do when
the storm is brewing over the horizon when the lead buffalo

starts to feel the lightning in their bones. At this stage in the leadership game, the leader who takes ownership understands that whatever happens from here on out is theirs. They are responsible for making decisions that will impact success or failure. From a position of ownership, a leader can organize tasks, motivate a team, create deadlines, and delegate accordingly, never tasking anyone on the team to do something that you, as a leader, are not 100 percent willing to do yourself. Taking ownership is understanding that you are committed to the entire journey and will lead through whatever the storm throws at you, all while protecting and using the herd.

Integrity Above All Else

As John and his Marines swept through a literal war zone, clearing houses of enemy fighters, he paid strict attention to how he and his Marines were behaving. "You aren't just responsible for the now, but you are responsible for what happens later. You need to know that you conducted yourself with the utmost integrity, discipline, and respect. Don't leave anything on the table that you are going to regret. We will live on values and not violence." This advice is pure gold in any leadership space.

Currently, I run a team that spans the entirety of North America. My team has a nine-digit goal with immense responsibilities and pressure for bringing in deals and building lasting business relationships with their clients. There are so many ways that corners could be cut to bring in something extra, and to be honest, it's unlikely that anyone would ever know about it—but that's not how we operate. This is what I tell my team each week. Integrity is like a bucket holding water. The water it holds is trust. When the bucket is fully intact, the water will stay in the bucket. As soon as you change the integrity of the bucket by poking holes in it or cracking it, the water (trust) will leak out, and the bucket will never hold the full amount of water ever again. You can patch the bucket up, but that will only buy you time until the bucket starts leaking again.

As leaders and people in general, we must maintain our integrity. Bending the rules or doing things halfway will inevitably hurt you and your teams in the long run. Leaders are doubly accountable because you now have ownership of your team, organization, or company. If your integrity is compromised, your team's integrity is compromised. Maintaining integrity is challenging. Here are a few ways to ensure that you don't poke holes in your bucket.

1) **Create a vision, mission, and core values:** Yes, every leadership book on the planet will tell you to do this, and that's why it's so important. You have to set a firm foundation of integrity that seeps out of your vision, mission, and core values. Create these *with* your teams. This will give them buy-in and create an unspoken agreement between you and them.

2) **Be honest in your communication:** Many times, your integrity can come under fire due to things completely outside your control. Whether it's a product misstep or a supply chain issue, problems will arise in the best of situations. As a leader, set the foundation of honesty in your communication. Let people know what's going on before they find out from somewhere else. Bad news never gets better with time.

3) **Set clear boundaries for yourself and your team:** Pushing yourself or your teams beyond the boundaries you establish can lead to violations of integrity. When you push beyond those boundaries, breaking the rules becomes easier. The extra task doesn't get the full attention it deserves, and the end state is incomplete. Setting

boundaries will help you and your team maintain the integrity of your work and your work ethic.

Note: This *does not* mean that you shouldn't stretch and challenge yourself and your people. This is a storm in and of itself, but it is healthy and necessary to push yourself outside of your comfort zone; that's not what I'm talking about here. What I *am* talking about is maintaining and communicating clear and established boundaries to ensure you can get a job done well.

Energy and Patience

When John and his platoon were about to demolish the building that the other Marines were in before they turned on their infrared blinkers, he was able to tap into his leadership training and make a decision that saved lives. His use of energy and patience diverted what would have been a disaster; it could have ended John's career. How can we use energy and patience when we're leading from the front?

Energy: The energy it takes to create a plan and make a decision shouldn't be taken lightly. If we aren't putting mental and physical energy into this process, the decisions we make won't be as complete as they could be. Leaders are faced with daily challenges, whether personnel, sales, business development, human resources, or any other part of the business. These challenges can be overwhelming. Each of them can turn into their own individual storm if we let them, but if we take a step back and tap into the problem-solving part of our brain, we can come up with the energy it takes to create a plan to solve any problem. What makes this process even better is when we involve our teams. Whether it's your direct teams or your peer groups, invite their energy into the planning process if possible. Two or three brains are always better than one.

Patience: Here comes the hard part. It has been said that an 80 percent solution put into action immediately is better than the 100 percent solution put into action later. I agree and disagree with this statement. To me, and I hate to say this, it depends. Yes, some decisions need to be made quickly; that's one of the best traits of good leaders. However, when there is time to be deliberate about a decision, it is always better to be patient in making that decision. Again, bring people into the process if possible. A patient decision, not a late one, will help reduce the possibility that you will have to return to this problem later. In John's case, if he weren't patient in his decision-making process, it would have been impossible to return to the problem and fix it. Fortunately, outside of the world of combat, we are allowed the luxury of patience in decision-making, as it is rare that an important decision will have to be made in less than a day.

I'll say it again: There is so much we can learn from John's story. He is a true American hero, an amazing leader, and a great friend. He leads from the front and ensures he and his people operate with the utmost integrity daily. John is now retired from the Marines Corps and is thriving, leading teams working on some of the most cutting-edge innovations meant to keep troops overseas safe, still leading from the front.

As motivating as John's story is, what happens when we have to take *ourselves* out of the fight? Leading from the front in Operation Phantom Fury taught us invaluable lessons about courage and resilience, but what happens when we must make outrageously difficult decisions to keep others safe and ensure we survive? As we move through our next storm, John's action steps will be crucial to survival. Our next leader, another outstanding Marine Corps officer, had to answer these questions and so many more. Our next storm will take us through the storm of mental health and the decision that she had to make to take care of herself and her Marines.

Operation Phantom Fury Pictures

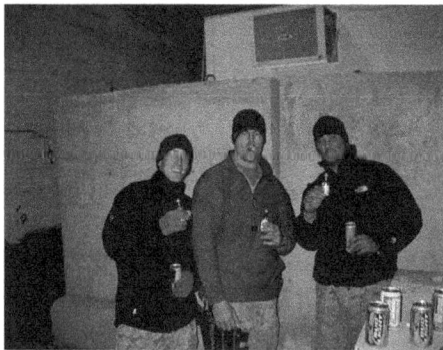

Operation Phantom Fury Pictures

Final Thoughts from John Bitonti

I am deeply grateful to Travis for the opportunity to con-tribute to this project and share my story, along with the stories of my brothers in arms. His dedication to capturing our experiences and ensuring they are heard is truly appreciated. Travis Hearne is a great American, friend, and fellow warrior Marine who is on a path that is dedicated to uncovering and preserving the remarkable stories of individuals and their experiences.

To my brothers in arms, it is only fitting that I extend my deepest gratitude to those whose extraordinary valor, unwavering dedication, and remarkable spirit have profoundly shaped the narrative contained within these pages. To the Marines and sailors of Company C, Warpig, of the 1st Light Armored Reconnaissance Battalion and the 3rd Light Armored Reconnaissance Battalion, you have my heartfelt apprecia-tion and respect. Your courage in the face of adversity, your steadfast commitment to our nation, and the sacrifices you made in service to the United States of America are nothing short of heroic. It has been both an honor and a privilege to lock shields with you in battle. The bonds forged through shared trials and triumphs in the harshest of conditions are unbreakable. The warrior spirit that each of you embodies is a testament to the strength of our military and the resilience of the human spirit.

The storm you faced in Fallujah was akin to a raging blizzard—relentless and fierce. Yet, like the buffalo braving the winter storm, you pressed forward with unyielding deter-mination and a commitment to the mission. The days and nights spent in the crucible of combat were marked by intense challenges and dangers. In those moments, your professional-ism, bravery, and selflessness were evident in every action and decision. The story of our time together is not just a tale of conflict but one of profound camaraderie and mutual respect. Your leadership, both on and off the battlefield, was a beacon guiding us through the chaos, and your sacrifice was a shield protecting us all. To my fellow Marines and Sailors, I am profoundly grateful for your sacrifice and for the privilege of serving alongside you. Your bravery ensured that I returned home safely to my family. My debt to you is immeasurable, and your sacrifice will forever be etched in my heart and memory.

As I reflect on our experiences and the indomitable spirit that carried us through, I am reminded of the profound bond we share—a bond forged in the fires of combat and tempered by the trials we faced together. Your unwavering dedication to each other and to our country exemplifies the highest standards of military service. Thank you for your valor, your sacrifice, and your unwavering commitment. You will forever hold a special place in my heart, and I am honored to call you my brothers in arms, my Marines, my Devil Dogs. I love you all. In closing, not a day, not one, do I not remember and honor those who made the ultimate sacrifice. Among them, LCpl Blake Magoay stands as a symbol of the bravery and selflessness that define our brotherhood. His sacrifice is a profound reminder of the costs of our mission and the depth of our commitment. LCpl Magoay's courage and dedication, along with the sacrifices of all our fallen comrades, will forever be etched in our hearts and minds. I love you and miss you brother.

6

THE STORM OF MORAL COURAGE: A STORY OF MENTAL HEALTH AND IMPOSSIBLE DECISIONS

This book is based on the analogy that the buffalo charges through heavy storms, weathering the onslaught of rain and snow and bringing the herd to safety on the other side, and that leaders have to do the same thing. What makes them even more unique to other herd animals is that the largest female normally leads the herds. She decides where to stop, when to go, when to rest, and when to eat. She leads the herd with wild yet careful precision through some of the toughest terrain known to man—or bison.

However, what happens when the herd leader gets injured or can't go on? What happens when the leader has to make the hard decision to let someone else take charge? What happens when we have to sideline ourselves in order to make ourselves and the people around us better? The storms of mental and physical health can be life-altering storms with the potential to destroy. Dr. Theresa Larson's storm could have destroyed her *if* she had let it happen. This is her story of survival, bravery, and moral courage.

Dr. Theresa Larson (aka "Dr. T") has become one of the healthcare and fitness world's most sought-after experts on movement, leadership, well-being, health, and longevity. Dr. Larson earned her doctorate in physical therapy from the University of Saint Augustine in San Diego, CA. Theresa also played professional softball in Italy and semi-professional softball in the United States and was an All-American Division I softball player at Villanova University and a former Body-for-Life Champion. Theresa founded Movement Rx with her husband in 2013 to break free from traditional physical therapy's limitations on practitioners and patients. Movement Rx is a company with skilled practitioners and speakers in the fields of leadership, mental performance, sleep, food, longevity, and movement. Her company works with the Veteran Administration, Center for Disease Control, and several corporate leadership teams, helping them dial in their well-being so they can increase their organization's engagement and improve retention and productivity.

In between all that, Theresa was a Marine Corps engineer officer and one of the few women to serve in a combat role during Operation Iraqi Freedom. Following in her brothers' footsteps, Theresa joined the elite ranks of Marine Corps officer. Here's a fun fact about female Marine Corps officers: They comprise only 4.3 percent of the Marine Corps officer demographic. To put that into an even broader context, less than 1 percent of the United States population serves in the United States Marines Corps. She was definitely one of the very few and the very proud. When Theresa joined the Marine Corps, she was going to break the mold for female Marine Corps officers. She aspired to join a reconnaissance unit and write a new chapter in the Marine Corps history books—one that included women in the most dangerous combat missions—and she was absolutely the one for the job.

Theresa finished OCS, TBS, and engineering school in 2003 and was sent to her first duty station at Camp Pendleton. As a female engineering officer, her second stop, after checking in, was with her brand-new engineering battalion. The anticipation of meeting the Marines she would serve with was inundating, nerve-wracking, and exciting all at the same time. This would be the crew she would deploy with and basically live with for the next three years; she desperately wanted to make a great first impression, but unfortunately, her car was in the shop.

Theresa, being without a vehicle but in a hurry, had to borrow her brother's truck to get to work on her first day. That may not seem like a big deal, but her brother was a Marine Corps C-130 pilot with an enormous, lifted, red, loud, bumper sticker-laden boss of a truck. It was an impressive piece of machinery but, stereotypically, driven by male Marine Corps pilots—with a huge emphasis on the male part of that equation—and Theresa's parking spot was right up front.

Now, don't get me wrong. Theresa is six feet tall and amazingly fit, but the truck didn't match the Marine driving, that's for sure. She squealed into the parking lot, revved the engine, pulled into her space, and shut down the red beast. She sat in the truck for just a second longer before meeting her Marines, as if the pressure of the situation just kicked in, thinking to herself, *I don't want to be seen as weak, and I don't want to be seen as attention seeking. I just want to do my job and lead well.*

After a few brief moments and some positive self-talk, she climbed out of the truck, slammed the door shut, and was quickly greeted by her new staff sergeant. "Hey, ma'am! You're my ma'am now! Let's get to know each other for a bit, and then I'll introduce you to the Marines." Theresa thought they would dive into conversations about explosives and building bridges—you know, engineering stuff. However, she quickly learned that the Marine Corps officer life would be different with this platoon.

Theresa recalls, "He started talking about all the problems the Marines were having. This Marine wanted to marry that one; this one wanted to become a nun; another just got in trouble, and so on. We didn't talk about a single thing that was related to engineering. I realized at that moment that a big part of my job would be taking care of the people I was in charge of. If we don't take care of our people, they can't perform well." Theresa knew she could help others, yet she was also young and had her own stuff she was working through. Either way, this was going to be hard, yet it was the hard she chose. She was determined to be the best at taking care of her Marines. At twenty-two years old, she was in charge of people who had problems a lot like her own, and it was now her job to take care of them so they could do their jobs well.

At this point in Theresa's career, she developed an immense passion for taking care of her people. She wanted to ensure they felt comfortable asking for what they needed, sharing about themselves and why they chose to be Marines, and asking for help if they needed it—a luxury that wasn't always afforded to Theresa later in her story, but we'll get there. Theresa was working hard to ensure everyone was taken care of, which was a tough and often unappreciated job, but her eyes were on the prize. She was going to crush this position and be one of the best officers in the Marine Corps, so much so that she placed a lot of her identity on perfection and achievement. On the outside, she was a machine, taking care of Marines and doing her job extremely well. On the inside, she was beginning to feel highly anxious and sometimes depressed—all symptoms she had felt before, yet this time it felt more intense. This time, feeling an intense need for control and struggling with her ability to cope, an eating disorder started to show its ugly head. This eating disorder would, in time, push her to her mental edge.

Theresa's platoon was preparing for their deployment to Iraq and was fully immersed in training and planning. Theresa began to build a reputation within the battalion as a badass. She was always on the top of the leaderboard in all the physical training, her Marines were squared away, and her platoon was always ready for anything thrown at them. However, Theresa's internal battle was beginning to become an issue. The external pressure she was under, which often left her feeling out of control, led her to take control of something nobody could take from her: her food. She developed Bulimia Nervosa, which meant that she would force herself to vomit after eating and abused exercise. This happened multiple times a day, but she hid it well. Nobody knew about it.

It came to the point that she had to tell someone about it, so she confided in her roommate, who referred her to a Doctor of Psychology she trusted. This doctor knew all about the disorder and how the Marine Corps handled things like this, and after a longer conversation, her roommate told her, "You can't tell anyone about this, or you won't be able to deploy." Theresa was left with two options. She could stay quiet and hide what was going on but still deploy to Iraq with her Marines, or she could speak up and try and get help but lose her Marines and the chance to lead them into combat.

Like many of us would have done and have done, she made the choice to stay quiet. In her mind, she couldn't let her Marines deploy to Iraq with someone else as their officer. That was an impossible thought for her at the time. So, she continued, thinking to herself, *I just have some eating issues. It'll get better when I deploy.* She pushed on with training, running, planning, and hiding her disorder from anyone and everyone.

A few months later, her dream came true. She was in Iraq with her Marines and was conducting combat operations as one of the first females ever to do so. She wasn't the kind to sit at a desk and give orders. She was a lead from-the-front badass who would never ask her Marines to do anything she wouldn't do herself. By day, she was on convoys and patrols, and by night, she was returning female detainees to their villages after interrogation. She was doing her job and doing it well. However, that didn't change the perception of the Marines around her.

Yes, a good number of Marines she was deployed with were happy to see her doing what she was doing, but it was uncommon and uncomfortable for many. Honestly, the stereotype of female Marines was the exact opposite of what Theresa was doing, even though, at times, she was doing a better job than her male counterparts. This sounds archaic, like something out of a World War II documentary, but female Marines were not seen outside the base. They usually ran the administrative side of the war behind the scenes, making everything run smoothly, but rarely in combat situations. It was extremely rare to see a female Marine officer on a convoy unless it was transitioning troops between bases. This was the unfortunate reality of combat from 2001 to roughly 2010. In 2003, an extremely rare group of badass women were pulled together to create Team Lioness. This small group of women was used early in Operation Enduring Freedom to answer cultural requirements prohibiting men from interacting with local Afghani women. Team Lioness would be the ones separating, questioning, and detaining, if necessary, any female combatants or local villagers. This group of women paved the way for the female engagement teams, which were established around 2009 and attached to each infantry battalion in Afghanistan. These roles comprised a fraction of the already small number of female Marines during the War on Terror years and were established after Theresa left the Marine Corps. Theresa was determined to be with her Marines and lead from the front, but as a female Marine Corps officer, that can be a lonely place.

Theresa recalled one convoy where she felt truly isolated, yet at the same time, unfairly called out. "We were on a convoy through Ferris Town, Iraq, and were attached to 1st Reconnaissance Battalion. It was a multi-day operation with well over one hundred Marines involved, so we took over a schoolhouse, staying there overnight. The schoolhouse had a huge gymnasium and a few empty classrooms. Most of the Marines were bunked up in the gymnasium. It made sense, and it's just how things were done. The junior Marines and noncommissioned officers would stay in the gym while leadership took the classrooms. Like any logical Marine Corps leader, I decided to sleep in the same classroom as *my* senior enlisted leaders. We'd been together for months now and built up a great relationship. But, since they were both men, the captain in charge of 1st Recon approached me and asked me what I thought I was doing. I said I was going to sleep in the same room as my enlisted leaders. We're in combat; what else would I be doing? Instead of listening to reason and trusting me as a leader, he forced me and two of my female Marines to take over the gymnasium and force at least thirty other Marines into other areas with extremely limited room. It made no sense whatsoever."

The deployment continued, and Theresa and her Marines participated in dozens of combat missions. She was still struggling with an eating disorder (that she still didn't want to admit she had), but she was doing her job well and pushed on. Her Marines were doing their jobs well, and the mission in Iraq was well underway. On the surface, things looked like they were going well, but the sting of declining mental health can hit you out of nowhere.

I want to caveat this because what I'm about to describe happened often in Iraq. Theresa was leading a convoy, establishing vehicle checkpoints in an active area of Iraq. This was no normal convoy. This was a fifty-vehicle convoy with over one hundred Marines. Theresa was in charge of getting this monstrosity from checkpoint to checkpoint, maneuvering along the dusty and IED-laden streets of Iraq. As she was trying to communicate with the entire convoy and with outdated technology and maps, somewhere along the way, she led the convoy in the wrong direction, straight into a dead-end along a one-way street.

Nobody was hurt, but Theresa had to figure out how to turn this giant convoy around and get them back on track. She recalled,

> I was trying to communicate with the convoy as best I could. My mind was on the mission, but my addiction was steadily creeping into my mind and clouding my decision-making ability. My mind wasn't fully there, and over a hundred Marines were counting on me to keep them safe. The truth is, I was not scared. I was battling hard to stay focused and present on my job—keeping my Marines safe and finishing our mission. We had done this dozens of times without incident. If we saw an IED, we called in EOD to take care of it, but that was just business as usual. When we returned to base that night, I knew something had to change. I was nowhere near 100 percent. My mind was on my Marines. They will go on, but someone else needs to do my job right now. They deserve better, and I need to get help.

This decision would change the direction of her career and her life. Malnourished from throwing up multiple times a day and fearing the worst, she walked into her commander's office and told him that she needed to see the command psychologist. What Theresa found out was that this disorder was not only misunderstood but also highly criticized. Each psychologist she spoke to didn't understand what she was going through and looked down on her for pulling herself out of the fight, even though it was the right decision for her and her Marines. She found that the great leaders she came to know and love were there for her, but there was a huge disconnect with those who were supposed to be caring and supporting her through this. "All of this could have been mitigated in a simple way. If they had gotten to know me from the get-go, we could have avoided this altogether. That's one of the biggest gaps we see in leaders today. They don't really want to get to know their people. They did not seem to care about me as a human being but rather a machine who went on missions and took care of my troops."

After not getting the help she needed or deserved in Iraq, Theresa was flown back to the US for what would be another round of judgment, scrutiny, and incredible misunderstanding of an all-so-common disorder.

In late 2005, Theresa was loaded into the C-130 to be flown out of Iraq, but the journey home would be anything but easy. With her on the plane were people who had been blown up, shot, hit with RPGs—you know, "combat injuries." She felt like a failure. "How could I have done this? Why did I take myself out of the fight? I let my Marines down."

As she landed at each base and spoke to psychologist after psychologist, the first question they all asked was, "Do you want to kill yourself?" She answered out loud, "No," yet in her heart, she was screaming, "Yes—maybe. I don't know. Why did I do this? My job was to be a Marine, and now, I'm coming home because of this!" Theresa was caught up in a mental tug of war—devastated that she decided to go home but, at the same time, knowing full well it was the right decision to make.

After Theresa returned to Camp Pendleton, she was ignored. As someone who was medically evacuated from a combat zone, she was supposed to be seen by the hospital immediately after she returned. However, after thirty days of being stateside, she called the hospital and demanded the help she deserved. Once again, leaders didn't understand. They couldn't wrap their minds around a Marine who would take themselves out of Iraq for an eating disorder. "They just didn't get it. If you have a problem with alcohol, you're given all the help in the world, but if you suffer from bulimia or another less commonly understood disorder, you are looked at like a leper."

After months of fighting for her mental health, she was honorably and medically discharged from the Marine Corps. She was beaten, grieving, and recovering from addiction, but not broken. She would not let her addiction take away her life or her future. She would engage in a healing journey that would take her to the deepest depths and the highest of highs, often wanting to give up but never doing so. This is where she gained a true passion and understanding for quality leadership and the value of holistically knowing a person. With her family in her corner, she embarked on an enduring healing journey. She started building a life where her mental, physical, and emotional health became a priority and where she would begin to change the leadership narrative around the globe.

Theresa was extremely close to her father. Her mother passed away years before she joined the Marines, so her bond with her father was unbreakable. She describes the messages that her father told her so many times, even in Iraq. Her faith in her father and the love he unconditionally gave her was why she asked for help. Over weekly tearful conversations, he would say to her, "The Marine Corps will go on. You might not if you continue to go down this path." Those words from her father were the encouragement she needed to get the help she deserved, and she holds onto those words to this day.

There are so many leadership lessons we can draw from Theresa's story; however, one of the most important discussions we can have about leadership is the conversation of mental health and making sure that leaders take care of themselves and their people. Let's unpack her story and pull out the action steps we need to successfully charge through the storms of mental health and lead ourselves and others in a healthy way.

ACTION STEPS

Leading Ourselves to Lead Our People

There is a price to pay for maintaining the health of a team. Often, the leader is the one who suffers. A study conducted by the Workforce Institute in 2023 showed that 35 percent of leaders are stressed, and 42 percent of these leaders say it's because of the pressure they put on themselves. Theresa's story proves this to be true. She put so much pressure on herself to prove people wrong, to be the best, and to show everyone that she belonged that it sent her down a path of destructive physical behavior. Her desire to be the best overshadowed her ability, at the time, to take care of herself as a leader. So, how do we do that? How do we take care of ourselves so that, in turn, we can take care of our people?

Surround Yourself with People You Trust

I think we've all heard the phrases, "Leadership is a lonely place" or "It's lonely at the top." I will say that leadership can get very lonely if you let it. Making decisions that will impact others' lives can often lead to isolation and loneliness. Sometimes, information needs to be kept from people to maintain a team's health. However, that doesn't mean that it has to be carried alone. The best leaders have people around them who they trust and who will call them out on their stuff when necessary. There is an old saying, "We are the average of the five people we spend the most time with." Here are some suggestions for how to find the people who will keep you operating and leading in a healthy way.

1) Find the top five trusted people in your life and create a board of directors for your health. This group of people is committed to your health as a leader and as a human being. They are people who don't work directly for or with you and people you could tell anything to.

2) Find people you admire outside your industry or workplace and cultivate a relationship. If you don't know them personally, find a way to reach out. One of the best ways to grow is to broaden your networks. Connection brings joy and learning.

3) Build up your internal champions within your workplace. Identify people with whom you can share your leadership burdens who will help you solve problems very tactfully. These people know your business and are committed to supporting you.

It's great to have people in your corner, but I have found that leaders tend to hold back their emotions and anything that could be considered "weak." The amazing Brene Brown states, "Vulnerability is the birthplace of love, belonging, joy, courage, empathy, and creativity. It is the source of hope, empathy, accountability, and authenticity."[2] I know this can get uncomfortable, but to truly work through the storms of mental health, we must be vulnerable with those who have committed to keeping us accountable for our health. I promise

---

[2]   Daring Greatly: How the Courage to Be Vulnerable Transforms the Way We Live, Love, Parent, and Lead by Brené Brown

you, as a Marine Corps Combat Veteran who was previously the most non-vulnerable human on earth, vulnerability is *not* weakness. It's the power that will unlock amazing success and long-lasting relationships.

Have the Moral Courage to Seek Help and Fight for Yourself

After coaching and consulting with leaders around the globe, one of the most common comments I get is that they are afraid to be seen as weak. Theresa was terrified of being seen as weak. That kept her from letting anyone know about her struggles and kept her from getting the help she needed that very well could have prevented her from having to come home. Corporate leadership is no different.

After the global shutdowns of 2020, mental health providers became overloaded with clients, which is good. However, in a shocking study conducted later in 2020, nearly half of Americans surveyed believed that seeking therapy was a sign of weakness. This is a stigma that needs to be obliterated. Those who seek counseling for ongoing stress or even for preventative maintenance have much lower levels of depression and anxiety. As leaders, if we are to lead our teams in holistically healthy ways, we must take our mental health into our own hands by seeking help when we need it. It's not a weakness; it's the strongest action a leader can take.

In Theresa's memoir *Warrior*, she quotes David Finkel, author of *Thank You for Your Service*, "It takes the courage and strength of a warrior to ask for help." Theresa showed amazing courage and strength by understanding that her mental health was getting in the way of leading her Marines. She knew she was putting their lives in danger by being there, and she took the necessary steps to protect them and get herself the help she needed. Because of that decision, she can empower high-impact leaders to do the same every day. Now, let's turn the page to taking care of your people.

According to numerous studies and articles published in the National Library of Medicine[3], *Forbes*, the Multidisciplinary Digital Publishing Institute[4], and so many more, a leader's mental health directly impacts the team's overall health. According to *Forbes* and the Work Health Institute, more than 70 percent of people in the workplace state that their leader has a bigger impact on their positive or negative mental health than their spouse or even their therapist. The impact that leaders have on those who follow them is undeniable, and to put a positive spin on this statistic, if a leader is mentally healthy, their teams are 70 percent more likely to be happy, motivated, and holistically healthy.

I'll say it again: Leading people is hard, and what makes it even harder is trying to lead from an unhealthy place. Theresa made the most difficult decision a leader can make. She knew she wasn't healthy enough to continue her current mission. Yes, she could have pushed through and finished the deployment, but that could have ended in disaster for her Marines and for her. As leaders, we have to look at the whole picture when making decisions that impact others. The decision to take herself out of the fight was one that came with scrutiny, judgment, and so many other negative things that unfortunately come with making decisions like this. However, what also came from her decision was long-term peace, advocacy for

[3] Vonderlin, R., Schmidt, B., Müller, G., Biermann, M., Kleindienst, N., Bohus, M., & Lyssenko, L. (2021). Health-Oriented Leadership and Mental Health From Supervisor and Employee Perspectives: A Multilevel and Multisource Approach. Frontiers in psychology, 11, 614803. https://doi.org/10.3389/fpsyg.2020.614803

[4] Paganin G, De Angelis M, Pische E, Violante FS, Guglielmi D, Pietrantoni L. The Impact of Mental Health Leadership on Teamwork in Healthcare Organizations: A Serial Mediation Study. Sustainability. 2023; 15(9):7337. https://doi.org/10.3390/su15097337

mental health, healing, and an example of morally courageous leadership. Theresa had to take care of herself to take care of her Marines. As leaders, we have to ensure we are holistically healthy enough to lead.

SECTION 1 CONCLUSION: STORMS OF SERVING YOUR COUNTRY

The leadership lessons that we can learn from the storms of military operations and combat are far more than I could put into one book. It's a different kind of leadership—one that only a few have the opportunity to experience—and it changes the way you view leading in the "regular" world. However, these lessons are highly translatable and useable in corporate, organizational, entrepreneurial, and any other leadership environment. The stress of making decisions isn't only experienced by captains and staff sergeants but by CEOs, individual contributors, and managers alike.

Storms of failure are probably the most common kind of storm but can also be the most devastating. To get through these storms, we have to take inventory of our emotions before we can start charging through them. Once we have overcome the negative self-talk, blaming others, and doubting ourselves, we can begin the process of regulation and healing and then move on to readdressing the problem, if possible. Once we've gone through all that, we write down the experience in a failure resume, so we have a record of what went wrong, what went right, and what we will do and not do next time, hopefully leading to success.

The storms of success can be two-fold. On the one hand, they could be a gentle and enjoyable rain that smells amazing, waters your grass, and gives you an opportunity to relax. On the other hand, success can be a driver for conceited action and self-worship. When we succeed, there is always something to learn, something to improve upon, and another opportunity just waiting over the horizon. In our lives, we are either going into a storm, battling in the storm, or coming out of a storm only to be thrust right back into another storm. Throughout this process, we have to take inventory of and learn from the storm, and if we are able to do that, we will find that we are far more prepared for the next blizzard.

Finally, leading people from the front isn't reserved for combat but in everyday leadership life. Leading this way builds trust and creates cultures of integrity and teams that can face anything together. Leading by example will show your people that you aren't afraid to get your hands dirty and that you, as a leader, aren't above anyone you serve. Be willing to jump in and do the work. It will help keep your skills sharp, and your team will follow you anywhere as long as your integrity is intact.

Without our integrity, we have nothing. Another piece of the bucket analogy is that it takes a long time to fill that bucket with trust but only seconds to empty it. As we lead our people, organizations, teams, and companies, remember that trust and respect are earned and never given. Regardless of title or position, we must earn respect from others because we are people with integrity and work ethic.

This journey through military leadership storms has been intense, but hold onto your hats. Our next series of storms are just as intense and can be just as devastating. Next, we will walk through the storms of the business world together. We will talk about organizational change, culture building, doing the impossible, and so much more. So, let's bear down, grab a few bites of food, shake off the snow, and get ready for the next round of storms.

SECTION 2

THE STORMS OF THE BUSINESS WORLD

7

THROUGH THE STORM OF CREATING AND MAINTAINING CULTURE: TRANSFORMATION AND GRIT

Yes, I'm going to say it because it's still a highly accurate statement. Peter Drucker said, "Culture eats strategy for breakfast." Culture building can be one of the most difficult things to do well, but when built, it is almost impossible to break. In December 2023, I was working for a large technology company and was tasked with creating a team that would be responsible for creating a brand-new go-to-market strategy for cybersecurity sales and business development. The company hadn't paid enough attention to our area of responsibility, and to be perfectly honest, we were losing billions of dollars to our competitors. This new team was meant to change all that. I was to scour the cybersecurity world and find the best nine people I could find to fill our North American business development team, and I had about a month to get it done.

The cybersecurity and tech world was in a state of turmoil regarding turnover. Companies were laying people off because of the over-hiring done during the COVID era and because of historic disruptions to the US and global economy. Conflicts between Russia and Ukraine, Israel and Palestine, supply chain issues, and political tension in the US led to a season of real difficulty for the cybersecurity industry and our country. Our company was re-organizing, which came with layoffs, change, and uncertainty. It was a storm that seemed to not only endure but also consistently change from pounding rain to blowing snow, to sunshine, and then back to rain with no end in sight. Yet we were determined to blaze through this storm and break new ground along the way.

The funding for my team came directly from our CEO's budget. This meant a couple of things. First, it meant that even in a resource-scarce environment, we would be given the necessary resources to get our jobs done well. Once the team was hired, our job was to be in front of our partners and customers, evangelizing our innovatively unique value proposition in a crowded security market. Second, it meant that we were going to be under a *huge* microscope. People in our company were being laid off, and I was given the budget to hire. Not only did we have to get this right, but we also had to do it fast.

The cybersecurity world was continuing to change, and we were already behind the eightball. We had to move quickly. With an amazing interviewing team established, we got to work. Over the next four weeks, we would interview forty-eight people, some multiple times. Our LinkedIn warriors were determined to find the right people, whether internal or external, for the job, and after a few close calls, the team was assembled. I had a team of nine rock stars spread across the US, Canada, and Brazil. After signing the last offer letter, I shouted, "Let's Go!" in my home office. It scared my wife a bit.

Now, we had a team. As individuals, they were all at the top of their game, but as a team, we were all rookies. We had never worked together, and as a remote team, we had never met in person. *What did I get myself into?* I thought. I was so concerned with hiring a bunch of individual professionals that I hadn't thought about how in the world I would lead this team. The pressure was on right out of the gate. I was responsible for reporting numbers, growth, establishing key performance indicators (KPIs), training the team, and sending them out into the wild to get in front of customers. We were charged with changing the way our company did business. This meant we had to create something different, and it all started with creating a culture that was different.

Earlier in this book, we discussed a significant failure I experienced. I've been lucky enough in my military and professional careers to have failed and bounced back multiple times. I was no stranger to being challenged. As leaders, we cannot be afraid of challenges. Yes, we may fail, but what if we succeed? What if we create something that sticks? What if we lead our team to unparalleled heights and success? What if we fail? What if? What if? That's the question we need to ask ourselves when we are faced with a challenge. What if? That simple question gives us the permission to take chances and provides the spark of motivation we need to get going. However, it all must start with building culture.

Creating military culture is much different than creating a culture within a company. The military is very macro-cultural, meaning that each branch of the military has very strict standards and procedures through which missions get accomplished. There is a ton of room for team building and camaraderie; there has to be. That's one of the main reasons for joining the military. However, the culture of the military, in general, is very hierarchical and established. Some will argue with me, but establishing a culture in a large company is different. But as a military guy, I couldn't just leave all that behind. I knew this team culture would need some guard rails, and it had to be grounded in theory. I am a leadership doctor, after all.

Transformational leadership theory is a leadership model that I have built dozens of teams upon. At its core, transformational leadership theory is all about leading individuals who will, in turn, transform your organization. As much as you can define a theory, transformational leadership theory is characterized by Langston University as "a leadership approach that causes a change in individuals and social systems. In its ideal form, transformational leadership theory creates valuable and positive change in followers with the end goal of developing followers into leaders."

As we dissect transformational leadership a bit more, getting into the blood type and bone marrow of theoretical biology, we find that the foundational principles are a leader's ability to foster an environment and create a culture in which their people feel individually considered, inspired, and motivated. The leader demonstrates and expects proper conduct within and outside of the boardroom (called Idealized Influence) and intellectually stimulates followers and the entire organization. The underlying core behind transformational leadership is that, when built on this framework, it can cement long-lasting and positive change within your people, increase their ability to lead, and change an entire organization for the better.

To understand the bones underneath the structural epidermis of transformational leadership, we must understand the man who corralled these concepts into theory. Dr. James MacGregor Burns codified the idea of transformational leadership in 1978 as the culmination of decades of research on political leadership. Dr. Burns was a Pulitzer Prize-winning presidential biographer and a pioneer in the study of leadership. He received his doctorate in government studies from Harvard University in 1947, later joining the Williams faculty, where he taught until 1986. Dr. Burns, whom many consider the grandfather of transformational leadership, led the teaching of this concept for forty years across the globe. Dr. Burns published dozens of books and empirically challenged articles on leadership from 1947 until he died in 2014.[5]

Before diving into transformational leadership and its immense value to culture creation, let's briefly get to know James MacGregor Burns. Before his Pulitzer was awarded and his academic and personal journey took flight, this man was a powerhouse—a literary mastermind with the ability to tell incredible stories about complex leadership situations. Knowing where Dr. Burns's leadership journey began gives us a clearer picture of why he was so emphatic about transforming leadership structures.

James Burns was born in Melrose, Massachusetts, in 1918 and was raised by his single mother. After completing his first round of academics at Williams College in 1937, he was drafted into the Army as a combat historian to serve in the Pacific during World War II. While enlisted in the Army, he studied the history of United States politics and military organizations and the different structures by which they were led. Here, it seems, is where the spark for transformational leadership began.

According to Burns' writings, whenever the terms "leadership" or "leader" were mentioned, only military officers were ever involved in the conversation. At the time, and even today, military officers were thought to be more educated and experienced than those enlisted. Burns saw this as a problem and verbalized his frustration with this concept early in his military career. He would go on to state, "In real life, the most practical advice for leaders is not to treat pawns like pawns, nor princes like princes, but all persons like persons," and that "Power wielders may treat people as things. Leaders may

---

[5] Williams College, Dr. James MacGregor Burns,

not."[6] If we bring these quotes into the context of his military service, we begin to see transformational concepts emerge.

The hierarchical constructs by which our political and military systems were led were not producing the best potential outcome for our country—and I would suggest they still don't. Furthermore, military leaders with incredible potential were being overlooked by the simple fact that their titles read "enlisted." Dr. Burns's time spent in the Army and on Capitol Hill began to shape his research. And thank goodness for that!

The focus of Dr. Burns's research revolved around the concept of transformational versus transactional leadership. He spent decades peeling back the onion of political and organizational leadership and how transactional it had become. Dr. Burns found that while necessary within certain constructs, such as military organization, transactional leadership was not conducive to long-term organizational or individual growth or success. Transactional leaders are hyper-focused on managing and supervising their employees rather than leading and challenging them. They are more interested in facilitating group performance through a performance-based leadership model rather than the personal growth of their people.

On the other hand, transformational leaders encourage their people to challenge the status quo and act as mentors. Motivation and inspiration are two essential tools used by transformational leaders, and they equip them to pull followers outside of their boxes and inspire innovative new ways of operating. The transformational leader knows who their people are and how they personally need to be motivated. These leaders use this knowledge to create a culture of inclusion while instilling an infectious sense of pride in organizational accomplishment. One of the outcomes of Burns's work was the four tenets, or pillars, of transformational leadership theory:

---

[6] James Burns, Leadership (ed. Harpercollins, 1978)

individual consideration, intellectual stimulation, inspirational motivation, and idealized influence.

Action Steps

Individual Consideration

We'll kick things off by talking about individual consideration. The tenets of transformational leadership are not meant to be a sequential list of boxes to check. Still, each one of them intersects with the other in many different ways and can be used to different degrees based on the leadership challenge. Individual consideration is very well defined by the phrase itself. It's the act of a leader listening and genuinely caring about what their people contribute.

It's a simple concept, but as we dive deeper into the context of individual consideration and its applicability in transformational leadership and culture creation, the definition becomes richer and has a deeper meaning. Individual consideration refers to "the degree to which the leader attends to each follower's needs, acts as a mentor or coach to the follower, and listens to the follower's concerns and needs. The leader gives empathy and support, keeps communication open, and places challenges before the followers (Langston University)."

Individual consideration is about respecting and celebrating followers' input and contributions toward actualizing the organizational vision and fulfilling the mission. Considering and acknowledging the personal accomplishments of your people will foster an environment where intrinsic motivation, based on internal drive, is commonplace rather than extrinsic motivation, which is based on transactional outcomes of success.

Intellectual Stimulation

Intellectual stimulation is a bit of a math problem (no pun intended) when leading teams of more than four people. Going back to and building on individual consideration, leaders must understand what intellectually stimulates their people. Larger teams will have more diversity in what intellectual stimulation looks like. One employee may want to go back to school, while another wants three hours a week to study and solve a work-related project of their own. This is where the communication piece continues to play a vital role.

Intellectual stimulation is the degree to which the leader challenges expectations, takes risks, and asks for and incorporates followers' ideas. An intellectual stimulator, that's the leader, encourages creativity and innovation, creating space for followers' ideas to flourish or even fail. This tenet is all about nurturing and developing your people as individual thinkers and creators. Let's look at a great example of using intellectual stimulation to transform an organization and an entire industry.

Dr. Edwin Catmull, the co-founder of Pixar and former president of Walt Disney Studios, started his career at his alma mater, the University of Utah (U of U), in their computer science department. Catmull was on the ground floor of groundbreaking experimental research in computer graphics in the late 1960s. At the time, the term computer graphics was as oxymoronic as jumbo shrimp or negative income. Dr. Catmull's research at the U of U was funded by the Advanced Research Projects Agency (ARPA), the organization that would eventually create what we now know as the Internet.[7]

Catmull's work with the U of U and ARPA was to develop a way to animate not with a pencil but with a computer. ARPA's mandate in all this was to "support smart people in a variety

---

[7] Ed Catmull, Creativity Inc., 2014

of areas" and was predicated on the belief that researchers would try to do the right thing and that overmanaging them was counterproductive. Dr. Catmull carried this mandate throughout his career, eventually expanding it in the creation of Pixar, sparking a cinematic revolution—one that was never thought to be possible. Dr. Catmull was given the freedom and intellectual stimulation to fulfill his computer animation goal, and television has never been the same.

This may seem like an uncommon example, but how do we know what our people are capable of without asking and giving them the opportunity to explore what that may be? Intellectual stimulation goes beyond giving employees challenging work. It is about digging into the core of what stimulates them intellectually, personally, and professionally.

Inspirational Motivation

I have to say that this might be one of my favorite tenets of transformational leadership. Inspirational motivation refers to how the leader articulates a vision that is appealing and inspiring to followers. Inspirational motivation is vastly different from situational motivation. Situational motivation is fleeting and based on quickly changing circumstances. Inspirational motivation endures because it is based on the vision and mission that the team put into place and has bought into.

A coach can motivate a ballplayer to win a baseball game, but once the ninth inning rolls around, their motivation changes from striking out the last hitter to the post-game pizza binge. If a coach is motivating a player to become a professional baseball player, the game literally and figuratively changes. The focus is no longer on the single game. It becomes something more. That coach's job is to inspire that player to work hard on and off the field, eat right, stay healthy, and do what he needs to do to help the team. This is what inspirational motivation is all about, and once again, it involves the leader getting to know their people.

Inspirational motivators consistently challenge their people with high standards, are optimistic about future goals, and show their people the value and meaning of the work being done. If you want your people to act, you have to motivate them in ways other than salary, bonuses, or other transactional ways. What intrinsically drives your people to get up in the morning? What really gets their gears moving? Why do they want to be here? It's a leader's job to move our people through a process of inspiration, the initial spark that gets someone to act, to motivation, acting upon that spark of inspiration, to discipline, a new operational mindset that is established as whatever inspired and motivated us is acted upon consistently. This creates a culture that is always growing and striving for excellence.

A great way to begin this process is by vision casting, creating your team's core values, and crafting a mission statement *with* the entire team. If the team is a part of this process, they will be that much more bought into the culture you are creating, and it will help them understand the reality that they are a part of something much bigger than them individually.

Idealized Influence

In the Marine Corps, our mantra was to "do the right thing, even when you think no one is looking." Idealized influence refers to how you conduct yourself as a role model and leader of character in the boardroom, on the Zoom call, and after hours. A leader conducts him or herself in a manner worth following. This pertains to how they speak, listen, act, and respond to their employee's needs, concerns, or complaints, as well as the storms of the ever-changing business world.

We have all been on that Zoom call when someone forgets to mute themselves. We start to hear the chatter that seems to have nothing to do with the actual conversation. Everyone else stops talking and looks to see who has the "hot mic." If you are sitting at the virtual head of the table, you frantically search for the mute button to ensure that your team member doesn't embarrass themself and that they don't say anything or have the team hear them say something they will regret.

This is an all too familiar occurrence these days. As leaders, we must live our lives, professionally and personally, as if our mute button is broken. The people we lead are watching us, listening to us, and analyzing our behavior. Leadership failures often bleed over into personal failures that could have been avoided. If you are to be trusted as a leader, you have to be holistically trustworthy.

We all have flaws and make mistakes. Even the late, great Steve Jobs self-admittedly made questionable leadership decisions at times. However, in a world where news and gossip travel instantaneously through social media networks, emails, and texts, we must ensure our leaders' behavior is above reproach. When we do make mistakes, we must address them appropriately and quickly.

Transformational leadership theory is a fluid process of knowing and communicating with your people. What we have to focus on throughout the process of incorporating these four tenets is that we are focused on organizational enhancement through the enhancement of our people. You may find these processes to be too loose and non-legalistic, but that's the point. If we, as leaders, are going to continue to steer our organizations toward success, it starts with the people. The main idea here is that if your people are nurtured to allow creativity, growth, consideration, and motivation, your organization will be more creative, considerate, and motivated, and your growth will surpass your expectations.

As leaders, we are the cultural torch bearers and the lead buffalo charging through the storms of creating something that will last; however, culture is a funny thing. Yes, it must be created quickly and intentionally, but it also has to be able to withstand the changes in the business. Culture should be mission agnostic, meaning that whatever task or challenge you and your teams are charged with accomplishing should be addressed with the team's culture top of mind. The actual plans you make and carry out to accomplish the mission will be unique, but the culture should be the catalyst for creating these plans. The best way I've found to accomplish this is by establishing the core values of your team. Here are the core values created by my team through the culture creation process. Since I'm a military guy, I created an acronym: Growth, Resilience, Innovation, and Trust (GRIT).

Growth

The first thing that must be understood is that the team is there to complete the job. This involves growing the business, the product, the idea, or the organization's message. For all of you Simon Sinek fans out there (I'm one, too), this is your business's "why." What was your team hired to do, and how do you exceed expectations in doing so? This part of growth is highly important because you won't be a team for long if you don't grow, but equally important is the individual growth of you and your team.

When creating a high-performing culture as a leader, you must consider the aspirations, dreams, and goals of the individuals on your team. This goes back to individual consideration. The best thing you can do as a leader is to create more leaders. Identify those on your team who want to take the next steps in their career and cultivate that. Don't be threatened by the strengths of those on your team. The best leaders are surrounded by people smarter than they are; I know I am!

Resilience

The buffalo can only brave the storm because of their incredibly thick skin. It keeps them warm when the snow thickens and the wind changes directions. As a team, you must be resilient. Whether you are a brand-new team or have been around for a decade or more, you will have to do hard things; otherwise, you wouldn't be necessary. This goes far beyond challenging business decisions. Resilience is about having difficult conversations with each other, listening to opposing views, sitting in uncomfortable spaces, and working toward the best possible outcome for the problem at hand. Circling back to idealized influence, the leader must be the most resilient buffalo in the herd. If you are having hard but healthy conversations with your team, you will create a trusting atmosphere where people can express their ideas and dissent from your ideas. When a team can have difficult conversations with each other and other stakeholders, problems can be solved quickly and efficiently. There is no time for inconsistent communication in the business world today. Leaders must create an environment where the team understands that these conversations are not personal and are based on the cultural vision that has been established.

Innovation

The buzzword of the twenty-first century. Yes, innovation is an overused term for change, but it's probably one of the most important keys to a successful team, organization, and company. If you aren't changing, you aren't growing. Challenge your team to take chances. Earlier, we talked about the importance of failure. It's vital to success. I would argue that there can be no success without failure. As a leader, give your people opportunities to try new things. Creating a transformational culture requires transformational and new thinking, so encourage your teams to think of things differently. As a sales and business development team, I bring in experts from other industries to help my people see other perspectives and ways of doing things.

Another worthy buzzword is diversity. If you truly want to innovate, you have to bring different people together. Bringing in a highly diverse group of individuals to solve problems creates new and innovative ideas that never would have surfaced had the group been from the same ethnic, social, racial, and industrial backgrounds. Diversity is extremely important when innovating. Encourage your people to branch out and broaden their networks to people who don't look or act like them.

Trust

Without trust, you don't have a culture. With trust, your team can overcome any storm. Trust and integrity are the foundation of any culture, whether at work or elsewhere. I tell my team often that we will be a team of integrity, or we won't be a team at all. We will be trusted advisors, resources, and people who can be depended on to tell the truth, even when it's difficult. Yes, this will involve having hard conversations, but again, this will ultimately lead to organizational, team, and individual success. This foundational value is the most important building block of your team's culture.

A tornado occurs when two opposing storms collide. The pressure from each of the storms throws them into a dance that eventually creates the funnel capable of destroying entire cities. The storm of culture creation is hard enough to blaze through, but what happens when something unexpected, like a pandemic, happens? What happens when an already overwhelming storm collides with another? What happens when you are trying to open a boutique hotel, unlike any hotel in existence, completely defying the hotel industry, and then a global pandemic historically changes the tourist industry and your entire life plan? Our next storm addresses exactly that, so let's use some of that thick, resilient skin and get moving.

8

THROUGH THE STORM OF SEEING THE LONG GAME: OPENING A HOTEL IN 2020

We are always either heading into a storm, going through a storm, or coming out of a storm. These three constants can beat us down if we let them, but what if we took this knowledge and looked toward the future? A herd of buffalo understands this well, so they immediately prepare for the next storm as they come out of the current one. They eat, rest, and heal from the previous storm with the knowledge that another one will come. They operate with the long game in mind. Now, what do I mean by long game? As leaders, we have to make sure we have a clear vision for the future and ask ourselves questions like, "What do I need to do now to ensure I succeed down the road?" and "Do I have the right people around me to brave the next storm that comes our way?" These are exactly the questions that Bobby Mikulas asked when he and his wife began dreaming of opening what is now one of the most unique hotels in the United States.

Kinship Landing is a boutique hotel in Colorado Springs, Colorado. It's not backed by any large hotel brands, which gave Bobby and his partners free rein to create something new.

It's smack dab in the middle of a bustling downtown area, surrounded by restaurants and bars, and has a breathtaking view of America's Mountain - Pikes Peak. However, before we jump into what Kinship Landing is, let's dive into the creation of the dream it was built on.

The story of Kinship Landing began when Bobby and his now-wife Brooke got engaged in 2009. One of the many things that drew them to each other was their equal passion for hospitality, travel, and anything cultural. They shared a hunger for the trails, peaks, valleys, and quirkiness of places they would visit, and soon, they would take their curiosity and passion with them overseas. "One day, before we have kids, we are going to travel the world," Bobby recalled. They would tell anyone they met that they were saving up enough money to spend at least a year overseas, and this, directly and indirectly, served as motivation to save up the cash and as an accountability mechanism to push them to execute their plan. If they told enough people about their plan, the execution was inevitable. Over the next seven years, they saved roughly enough money to make their plan a reality.

As wild and spontaneous as this trip would be, Brooke and Bobby are leaders through and through. So, as great leaders do, they began to organize and structure their trip into three phases: rest, dream, and plan. They would build their entire year around these three concepts and hold each other accountable to the process within each phase.

Bobby is a visionary and a passionate ideas guy, and on day three, Bobby said to Brooke, "Oh, man! Wouldn't it be amazing if we could..." Bobby began dreaming about the future—but that wasn't part of the plan, so Brooke, being the disciplined human she is, gently brought Bobby back into the rest phase of their journey. "Can you knock it off with the ideas? We are resting right now," Brooke reminded him. And with the reality of rest fully embraced, they spent the first three months of their trip enjoying the hospitality of strangers and resting well.

After their hearts, minds, and bodies were restored, and much to Bobby's delight, the dream phase began. This was the phase in which they would throw around wild and practical ideas that would set up their planning phase. They talked about which country they wanted to live in, how many kids they would have, whether they even wanted to have kids, what kind of community members they wanted to be, and what they should do whenever they got to where they wanted to land. They dreamed about everything but found that they truly enjoyed getting up close and cozy with people from all walks of life from all over the world. They would observe different cultural parenting styles, how children were cared for, healthcare, education, and how different people lived their lives. They immersed themselves in the communities around them, often staying in people's homes and eating their food. Their dreams were fueled by the experiences they were living, and their plans would be built off the widest variety of wisdom they could attain. You couldn't get this information from a book; you have to live it.

As their yearlong excursion across the globe continued, so did their dreaming. They knew they would eventually have to come to a place of agreement about where they would live and what they would do. They questioned, "Should we open a child development center in China or move back to Colorado and build a real estate company? Should we take what we've learned and start taking people on adventures all around the world?" The entire world was open to them. They just had to decide what to do and put all their effort into doing that thing, but it wasn't that simple.

Brooke and Bobby had a general idea of what they wanted to do. They decided, partially to Bobby's chagrin, that they would come back to Colorado and create something based on the culture of Colorado Springs, but that was about it. Bobby often says, "Some people see Kinship Landing as it is today and think it's the culmination of this ultimate vision that we had, but that couldn't be further from the truth. But what did emerge was a clear passion to bring a new kind of hospitality to our hometown."

They had always been drawn in by the different cultures around them, from the foreign exchange student to the construction worker who didn't speak English. They were fascinated by ways that they could be hospitable to diverse cultures and wanted to bring this fascination to the world, but their ideas were anything but corporate.

Bobby's idea of this kind of hospitality is what he calls "backyard and mountain hospitality." You invite someone who doesn't look or sound like you into your home and share a meal around a table or a campfire. Throughout the first six years of their marriage, they continuously had anywhere from two to ten people living with them at any given time, and what they found out during this time was that there was a need in Colorado Springs. There was a massive influx of tourism in town, a lack of infrastructure to support them, and a lack of intention to connect these tourists to the best of the community. This was the spark of something great, but what would it be? A good friend of Brooke and Bobby would ask them the question that would move them down the path leading to Kinship Landing. That question was, "What are you uniquely qualified to do that no one else can do to the level or style you can?" When they answered this question and overlapped their answer with the identified need, they created the loose idea of some high-end hostel in downtown Colorado Springs and began planning.

After refurbishing a van into a camper, they spent the last three months of their trip in New Zealand to begin the planning part of their journey. They began working out their business plans, vetting business partners, and socializing their plans with anyone who would listen. They were going to bring a new kind of hospitality to Colorado Springs. "Our version of hospitality will be informed by some of the best and most unique places around the world. It will be informed by the outrageous hospitality that we have been the recipients of. It's the crazy, gracious act of being generous when nothing has been done to earn it except for showing up and being there. Where people just bend over backward to make your time extra delightful, extra comfortable, extra authentic, and real." Furthermore, they wanted to create a space for locals to interact with out-of-towners in a symbiotic and harmonious way, sharing all the hidden nuggets of their city with each other and finding a place where they felt welcomed. Once they knew what they wanted to build, they headed home.

After arriving back in Colorado Springs, they got busy learning. Brooke and Bobby would attend every free consulting event they could find and enroll in anything that would help them learn about what they were going to build. They had their vision, but the next step was bringing the right people alongside them. In order to actualize their vision, not their single-year or even two-year vision, but their ultimate vision, they started identifying the team with which their dream would become a reality. Bobby's game plan for creating this team was very intentional. He wanted long-term employees and partners who were 100 percent bought into the Kinship Landing vision. He and Brooke would identify gaps that needed to be filled and would recruit people to fill those gaps. Once he found the right people to fill these gaps, he would focus on inspiring and motivating them toward the ultimate dream. "That's the hard work of a leader, not doing all the work like swinging hammers and building the hotel, but equipping, inspiring, and motivating the right people to do the work and align that vision."

Over the next few months, Bobby, with a team of partners, friends, and consultants, created a team, business plans, and financial modeling to build Kinship Landing. This was in 2017.

As Bobby and his team got to work on making this hotel a reality, they came up with their five core values: courage, trust, community, generosity, and adventure—and they were socializing these, along with their business plan, around Colorado Springs to anyone who would listen. The team went into a full-court press identifying investors, potential properties, and anything else that would make their dream come true. Once again, just like their trip around the world, Bobby and the team spoke about Kinship Landing as if it were a certainty.

Often, luck, chance, provision, or whatever you want to call it plays a huge part in success, but to respond to that lucky moment, you have to be prepared. In a meeting with the Colorado Springs Chamber of Commerce, those values struck a chord with one of their leaders, who then pointed them toward a local developer, saying, "I don't know why, but I want you to meet this woman. I don't know if it will go anywhere, but I'll at least make the introduction." She had been building apartments downtown and was in the middle of a project herself, so the team set up a meeting.

A week later, Bobby and his team met with the developer. Bobby was looking for a building and was hoping that this developer could point them in the right direction of something downtown that they could refurbish or renovate, but as life does, she threw him a curveball. About forty-five minutes into the meeting, she said, "I don't know of any pre-existing buildings in the area, but do you see that empty plot across the street? That one's for sale." Bobby and the team looked over at the lot with wide yet careful consideration. They never thought of building something new. Their development plans and the money they had spent so far were leading them toward a renovation, not a new build. The developer mentioned what the price would be for the land, and immediately, Bobby rebutted, "No, we can't pay that, but I would love for you to take the weekend and think of the lowest possible number that you would be comfortable with and let us know." They shook hands, swapped phone numbers, and parted ways—Bobby with the new possibility of recreating his plan and the developer with a financial decision to make. The land was in a perfect spot, but would the price be right?

After a few days of nail-biting and re-dreaming, the developer called with her number. The phone rang, and with bated breath, Bobby answered. After a few seconds of pleasantries, she gave them her number. Shockingly, the number was well under Bobby's anticipated bottom line, and without hesitation, he said, "Yup! We're in!" They were pumped. They were under contract on a piece of land that would host their vision and visitors from around the world.

As the contracts were drawn up and realtors looked them over, they found something that could dramatically halt the entire thing. They were going to have to close on the land in thirty days. Yet again, another wrench was thrown into the mix. After hoping and asking for a ninety-day extension, the developer wasn't budging, so they had to figure something out quickly. The team jumped into action, calling everyone they could get ahold of to get soil samples, architectural designs, and everything else they would need to close on this sweet piece of earth in the heart of downtown Colorado Springs.

It was crunch time! The money for the land was due, and they were quickly running out of capital to start the project. Bobby and the team did as much fundraising as possible, but they were falling drastically short. "We weren't sure what we were going to do, but we knew this was the dream, so we had to make it happen."

They were a significant amount of money short of closing on the land within thirty days when, once again, fate would take over. Bobby, being the open book that he is, had a random conversation in a hot tub with a friend about the hotel and how they were financially falling short on closing. Without much hesitation, this friend said, "Well, what if I lend you the money?"

Bobby was shocked. He never considered a loan before because he didn't think it was possible. "Wait, you have that kind of money to lend us?" he asked.

His friend responded, "Yeah, I love the vision and what you guys are creating. Let's do this!"

So, thirty-three days after having a conversation with a stranger about a piece of land, it was theirs. They closed and began the construction process.

It was a miracle they could pull this all together so quickly, but that was just the first hurdle. With an unforeseen pandemic unknowingly looming just around the corner, they moved as quickly as they could to start digging and continued to raise as much money as possible. Over the next two years, Bobby would have to build a team. He knew that he wasn't going to hire the actual staff of the hotel until 2019, but the vision had to sustain them throughout the building process. After all, he had investors, a wife, and a town depending on him to build Kinship Landing.

Over the next few years, Bobby would inspire and motivate the people around him to actualize their dreams. Bobby's idea of inspiration and motivation went like this. "Inspiration and motivation are two completely different things. I can motivate someone by punishing their actions if they don't succeed and rewarding them if they do. Inspiration is something you can't stop thinking about. You wake up excited to do it. If you take away external motivating factors, you are left with the inspiration that drives you forward." I completely agree with what he says here. He was able to provide his team with the inspiration to carry on and build this hotel, working through adversity and blessings at every turn.

Everything was starting to come together, and then a global pandemic would shut down the world. Bobby and the team were about to build a boutique, startup, non-flagship hotel during the worst-on-record hospitality event to ever occur—to say that things turned quickly is an understatement. Three days before the groundbreaking ceremony, the bank pulled their funding. They lost most of their financial backing for their dream three days before the mayor was going to help Bobby and Brooke put golden shovels into the ground, and they were sure their investors would be next. It was just too risky. They began calling everyone involved to inform them about what happened. Logically, some investors backed out, but miraculously, more investors jumped on board. They decided to move forward with the groundbreaking ceremony, so with the mayor, city councilmen, investors, and media all gathered over their plot of dirt, they officially broke ground—without a bank to back them up.

Once ground was broken, they had no choice but to pause construction for six months while they found another bank that believed in their long-term vision. This was when the storm hit. One of the reasons the bank pulled out was because they were dramatically over budget. They would have to go back to the drawing board on design, construction, architecture, interior design everything. At the same time, Bobby had to find another bank and more investors and keep his team inspired enough to keep pushing forward. They gave their investors an out. "Here's the deal. We need to reshuffle the deck, but we're offering you your money back. We'll sell the land if we have to, but we want to do right by you since you believe in the dream. We're offering ownership of the company. If you stay with us on this, you'll be an owner of Kinship Landing."

Almost every investor they had onboard chose to stay in the storm with Bobby and the team. Even though everything seemed to be stacked against them, the team believed. They believed in the vision and the dream and were all in. Not only were the investors all-in, but they also found a bank that believed in them. They were back on track, and construction began.

In December 2020, in the middle of a global pandemic, Kinship Landing was about to open its doors. The architecture was unlike any other hotel out there. Bobby and Brooke created their hotel to be unlike any other in the industry. They created rooms where you could pitch tents on the oversized patios, bunk rooms that could sleep eight people or more, and king suites that were as luxurious as any other mainstream hotel with a restaurant that created the best cuisine imaginable. They hired their skeleton crew, chef, night auditor, and assistant general manager. They were ready to go. Then, construction delays on the main level forced them to postpone the opening two months.

The team had to cancel reservations, push back their marketing efforts, and reject much-needed revenue. This took the wind out of their sales. They were opening a hotel during a pandemic—doing something nobody else was doing—and were now stifled by construction. Bobby once again had to jump in and inspire and ensure his team. "This is part of it. We are in this. We aren't going anywhere, and nobody's getting fired. We will open, and people will love this." Bobby's level of inspiration jolted the team forward, creating a warrior mentality within them. They were even more gung-ho than before.

Construction delays weren't going to push back their opening any longer. Although their main level wasn't finished yet, Bobby opened the hotel and welcomed guests in January 2021. Since the main floor was still incomplete, they created a make-shift check-in area in one of the elevators. Guests would check in through one elevator and then take a few steps to their left or right, hop on the other elevator, and get to their rooms. Their dream was finally a reality.

The pandemic eventually faded, and the hospitality industry made a comeback. Kinship Landing is now one of the most sought-after hotels and restaurants in Colorado Springs, playing host to people from all over the world. This story began with two twenty-somethings dreaming while they traveled the world and was transformed into an actual building where cultures collide and people from all walks of life gather to share meals, drinks, and rooms. Bobby and Brooke continue striving to enhance and support the culture, and delivering their vision remains on track, ensuring their dream remains pure and people are taken care of.

ACTION STEPS

The origin story of Kinship Landing is filled with years of overcoming some of the most devastating storms a business can endure—a global pandemic, banks backing out, investors leaving, relationship dynamics, hiring, firing, and so many more. Seeing and believing in the long game was the guiding light that got Bobby and his team through these storms. Bobby created a culture out of his belief that they would open this hotel and inspired his team and the people around him to believe in him.

Overcoming Failure

When creating something new, we must keep the long game in mind. The first lesson we can pull from Bobby's story is to never let failure dictate our success. If we are going to create something great, we will fail along the way. I talked about my failure earlier, but I want to reinforce this theme.

If Bobby had let the storm of failure overcome him, Kinship Landing would never have been built.

As you build or create something new, understand that failure comes with the territory. Don't let this stop you. As I said before, learn from your failure, take notes, and try something new. In the case of Kinship Landing, the mistakes that were made helped create what Kinship is today, and without them, it wouldn't be the same. I understand that opening a boutique is a much larger scale problem than most of us face on a day-to-day basis, but overcoming failure will help you succeed in everything you do in life and in leadership.

Believe in Your Dream

Bobby repeatedly spoke about believing in your dream and telling everyone you know about it. This may seem a bit overconfident, but speaking about your dreams as if they are 100 percent going to happen will drive you toward success. He inspired people with the *idea* of Kinship Landing, and that boldness turned into investors, champions, supporters, friends, and eventually customers. Be bold in your vision and create it as if it were certain to happen.

Culture is Key

As you choose people to go on any professional journey with you, hire for culture and train for skill, but find a good balance. Bobby said in our interview, "When we hired for culture, sometimes it didn't go right, but it turned into a story, a lesson learned, or a laugh. When we hired for skill, if it didn't go well, it would end up in a lawsuit." When people buy into your vision and fit into your culture, you can train them to do the work—as long as their skillset at least ticks most of the professional boxes.

Inspire People Through the Storm

Constant inspiration, a little bit of structure, and action-able steps forward are the foundation of building a great team. If you can get people onboard and inspire them with your vision, they will be amazing allies in your journey. If you can inspire them with your vision and your actions, they will go into the eye of any storm with you. You have to go beyond motivating your people and inspire them to be great.

P.S. You can't fake vision. It needs to be something you can see and believe in your bones will come to pass.

Don't Be Afraid to Get Your Hands Dirty

Before Kinship Landing opened its doors, Bobby and Brooke linked up with another hotel in a different city and shadowed employees from every department. They were house-keepers, cooks, front desk clerks, general managers, janitors, and everything in between. As leaders, we have to be hands-on with the work and pass on the knowledge we gain to our people. Don't be too afraid or mighty to roll up your sleeves and finish the work.

Don't Forget to Dream

Our last action step is to continue to dream big dreams. Our world is so caught up in progress and quick wins that we can forget to dream about what we truly want out of life. We can get caught up in the storm of complacency and never get out. If we learn nothing else from this storm, it is that we have to dream and speak about our dreams as if they are a reality. To survive the storm of the long game well, you must be equipped with dreams, goals, and the enthusiasm to go after them. You never know. You may just actually make your dream a reality.

While much of this story is told in consideration of Bobby and his wife, Brooke, he will be the first to point out that the success and vision of Kinship is the direct result of a massive community of stakeholders. Not the least of these are three brave co-founders who jumped on board with Bobby and Brooke in the very early days, rode the rocky startup road, solved problems, and took massive risks together. The fingerprints, commitment, and expertise of other co-founders, community members, investors, and more cannot be overstated. Bobby, Brooke, and their teams braved many storms as they actualized this stage of their dream. One of them wasn't unique to them, their industry, or even Colorado Springs. When a global pandemic sent all of us into our living rooms, a new storm began to circulate. Every industry was impacted by the COVID-19 storm, including leaders of companies and teams. Many of us were thrust into a hybrid and remote work world, and leaders had to figure out how to lead their teams from their kitchen tables. Our next storm came upon us without warning and without training. It has forever changed the business world. It's a storm that could either lead to green pastures or rocky ridges. It's starting to snow, and the herd is getting anxious.

FINAL THOUGHTS FROM BOBBY MIKULAS

When I was younger, I encountered Love. That relationship grew, and it is because of Jesus that I am free and empowered to dream and act with the conviction that it will be okay, that big ideas are possible, and that it's not up to me. Thank you, Jesus.

Thank you with my whole heart to my partner and bride, Brooke Mikulas. It is because of Brooke that I find my way when I get lost, that I am afforded the opportunity to take risks, and that the best ideas are recognized and championed.

My parents nurtured my character and identity in a way only great parents can, a provided model worth following. Thanks, Mom and Dad.

To the too many to count friends and mentors; thank you for choosing to spend some of your precious time seeing me, having fun together, and giving me a chance to level up.

As it relates to Kinship Landing, there are too many people to thank here. My founding partners are at the top of the list. Kinship was Brooke's idea and vision, and her tolerance for risk, hard work, and perseverance got us to where we are. Her creative eye, care for people, and attention to detail will endure in what we built together. Nate, thank you for your expertise, willingness to jump in, and creative problem solving. You stuck in there when others would have bailed and offered plenty of brilliance to the mix. Jason, who you are as a person kept us on track with our values when we were tempted otherwise, and we would not be here without you.

Loren, you were the first one to see that we had something worth taking very seriously. Thank you for sharing your wisdom, energy, and your friends in the most generous ways. To our investors, thank you. You saw beyond what was certain into a community asset that needed to happen. Thank you for your commitment to the journey and your loyalty. To

Ryan Lloyd, Sara and Troy Derose, and Jay Gust, thank you for putting your fingerprints and heart into something that was not yet real. And to all the people attached to the story; our team led by Lindsay, our friends, neighbors, guests, and advocates, thank you for being the reason Kinship is a new kind of hospitality, where people make the place.

We have one life to live. Go for it!

9

THROUGH THE STORM OF CHANGE: NAVIGATING THE REMOTE WORK REVOLUTION

Since the pandemic of 2020 shut down the world and sent the workforce into their living rooms, leaders have struggled to understand how to lead in this new normal. Our work lives are forever changed—relationally, economically, physically, structurally, and in almost every possible way. This new storm that only a few leaders had experienced previously is seemingly here to stay. Many of us were waiting for our new normal to begin or for the comfortability of lives once lived to return, but now, we have to realize that remote and hybrid work is here to stay. We must *create* our new normal. As businesses and organizations morph into a new and exciting model of their previous selves, leaders have to learn how to adapt and flourish through the storm of leading virtual teams. Businesses, small and large, must create a new way to thrive, scale, lead, manage, and change with new hybrid and remote workforce.

Hybrid and remote work are hardly new concepts. In 1999, the *Wall Street Journal* reported that more than half of companies with over five thousand employees used virtual teams with leaders spread out across different areas of the country.[8] Martins, Gilson, and Maynard predicted that the virtual work environment trend would increase as it became more technologically efficient and more financially beneficial.[9] What was not accounted for was a global pandemic that would force businesses, government institutions, and otherwise "business in-person" organizations to embrace a new virtual leadership reality. As of September 2021, corporate giants like Apple, Cisco, Ford, Microsoft, and Target have moved to a permanent, hybrid workforce, allowing employees to choose how and where they want to work. The world of corporate leadership and management has changed forever. Leaders must be equipped with the correct tools to progressively change with the times and lead and manage hybrid and remote teams.

I want to establish a baseline before we get too deep into this storm. Leadership and management are two wildly distinct, however tightly intertwined, concepts. Both are difficult to do well, even under the most pristine and unchallenging circumstances. Throw in a policy that forces you and your entire staff out of the cubicle farms and corner offices and into the basement, and the difficulty multiplies dramatically. It's like throwing water on an already wonky machine and expecting it to not only work correctly but also perform even better than before. Before we can begin to discuss how we will move into a bright future of leadership in a hybrid environment, we, unfortunately, need to briefly relive an impactfully painful moment in recent history that forced the global economy into an unimaginable and heartbreaking season of change.

Carl Sagan stated, "You have to know the past to understand the present." So, let's go back to November 2019—a

---

[8]   De Lisser, The Virtual Office, Wall Street Journal, 1999

[9]   Martins, L., Gilson, L., and Maynard, T., Virtual teams: What do we know and where do we go from here? (2004)

simpler time. The United States presidential election was the sole focus of media outlets across the globe. Our televisions were inundated with debates, campaign commercials, talks of impeachment, and waves of civil unrest following numerous and unimaginable tragedies actively dividing our country further.

Behind the scenes, it seemed, was a war in Afghanistan waged with no realistic end in sight, surpassing its twentieth anniversary. While these tragic realities cut and nipped at the American fabric, most Americans did what they do best: They took care of each other. Unemployment hit a record low, and we celebrated the women's American Football (Soccer for us Yanks) World Cup victory. NASA successfully conducted the first-ever all-woman spacewalk, and the Washington Nationals defeated the Houston Astros, winning their first-ever World Series title.

The world (and space) was still spinning. There were no mask or vaccine mandates, restaurants were packed, schools were open, concerts were kicking, and it was a golden era of easily traveling around the world. We Coloradoans were ecstatic about what *The Farmer's Almanac* called a "Polar Coastal Winter," meaning feet of fresh, skiable powder would soon fall on Summit County.

The news cycle continued to buzz with an almost white-noise kind of consistency when, all of a sudden, things began to shift. The white noise changed from elections and civil unrest to coverage of the first case of a rare and highly contagious virus in Wuhan, China. Like many of you, I initially watched this unfold with tangential apprehension at best. I felt deep concern for the people of China, but I was sure that this would be a controlled incident, as we had seen in previous outbreaks. There's no way it would make it all the way across the globe—or so we thought.

In March 2020, the World Health Organization declared COVID-19 a global pandemic, shutting down borders across the globe and causing most global industries and businesses to grind to a dramatic and immediate halt and shutting down international borders. The S&P 500 took a 30 percent plunge, and by May, the US unemployment rate hit 14.7 percent, the worst rate since the Great Depression, with 20.5 million people out of work—a dumbfounding shift from only a few short months before. Four months turned into eight, and eight turned into twelve, and it became our national priority to "flatten the curve."

The global economy was changed forever. At the time, I was working as the chief interagency and operations officer for an element of the Department of Defense responsible for defending the Homeland. Our job was to ensure that the United States, Canada, and Mexico were protected from several threats and vulnerabilities, a gargantuan task. For the year and a half leading up to the pandemic, our mighty fifteen-person rockstar of a team was as tight as one could get. The flow in which we worked never seemed overwhelming. Our people had an outstanding work-life balance, and they seemed to be very happy with their jobs.

Then, in March 2020, my inbox began to overflow with messages from the commander's office. The first batch of emails ordered us to go down to 50 percent manning. I thought, *Okay, we can still do that. We could cut down their daily hours using some fancy human resources tools and make that work.* We would cut the team in half and split up a twelve-hour workday. Easy peasy! By the afternoon of that same day, we got the notice from our four-star commanding general that our three-person leadership team was the only team allowed in our offices (a space built for fifteen), and the rest of our team would have to begin working remotely immediately.

We had to split a twenty-four-hour day into three separate shifts while only overlapping by thirty minutes. How, on earth, were we supposed to do our jobs? We were the Department of Defense; being able to do our work effectively was *literally* a matter of national security. How would I ensure the homeland defense boulder was continuously pushed uphill while we completely changed the environment in which we worked?

So, as any good Marine would do, I leaned on my previous training and created a plan so great that it would fail four times before it actually worked. I started with a virtual meeting rotation three times a day. Fail. Okay, how about once a week? Fail. Fine, we will meet on Monday and Friday. Fail. After banging my head against the wall for about two weeks, I realized I needed help. I had never had to figure out a problem quite like this; I had to turn to the experts on this one. I looked at myself in the mirror and said, "Okay, all those failures have to be some sort of playbook for success, right?"

I started digging into every leadership and organizational change book I had collected over the years and looked for help. I needed to look at this problem through the eyes of Dr. Urie Bronfenbrenner, Dr. James Burns, and Dr. James Kotter. I poured over Dr. John Maxwell's literature on leadership and change. There had to be something in all this foundational leadership and change theory that could be used to answer the organizational calculus problem I was handed. The good news was that there was more material on organizational change and leadership than I could ever fully understand. The bad news was that there was more material on organizational change and leadership than I could ever fully understand. Again, leaning on my Marine Corps metaphors that I was so proud of, I began to size up this massive hill that I was about to take, game planning on how to blaze through this storm as the head buffalo. But now, I had the ammunition I needed to get the job done.

Theory in hand, I began to ask questions of my staff, listen to their concerns, and watch as this calculus problem turned into basic math. My focus had to be on my people, what they needed during this intensely stressful period of history, and how we could best work together toward mission accomplishment. Earlier, we talked about culture building. I would have to recreate a team culture in a remote work environment that was completely foreign to me. It wouldn't look the same, but it had to work. Here are the action steps I took to blaze this new trail through a storm that had never been seen.

ACTION STEPS

Set Clear Expectations

Remote and hybrid leaders don't have the luxury of popping into offices or cubicles daily to check on how our people are doing. Since that is the case, setting clear expectations is the first part of driving your team toward success. It will ensure they know what is expected and give you clear metrics on how to evaluate them in the future. By specifically defining roles, responsibilities, and expectations for each of your people, you are giving them the autonomy to get the job done wherever they may be working.

This seems like a no-brainer for all teams, but it becomes even more important when you aren't present with your team every day. Establishing clear communication guidelines, including response times and deadlines, regular one-on-ones, and simple daily check-ins, becomes a way to re-humanize a dehumanized workplace. The better defined your expectations of your individual team members are, the less this storm will impact you and your team.

Leverage Technology

In a remote world, technology is your best friend. Without it, you cannot lead your team, but the problem is the number of options that address the different elements of leading remote and hybrid teams. There are video conference tools, instant messaging tools, email, project management, collaboration, file sharing, time tracking, task management, and the list goes on and on.

To determine which tools you need, you must understand your team and individual workflow. As a guy who's been leading remote teams for a long time, I recommend finding one standard platform and using every widget it has. Bringing in different types of software with different dashboards and options will make things more complicated and confusing. Keep it simple and find a single vendor or solution that will address most of your needs.

Build Trust and Inclusion

Using the GRIT framework discussed earlier is a great way to build team culture. However, it can't stop there. As leaders, to continue to build trust and ensure each of your team members feel like they are a part of a team, we must be accessible and transparent with our communication. There's nothing worse for a remote team member than having to guess what is going on with your organization, department, or even your own team. Remote work can get very lonely. Leadership must go above and beyond in their communication to ensure that the most up-to-date, helpful, and relevant information is given to the team.

Now, I said helpful in that sentence. What I mean by helpful is this. You don't have to tell your team everything. One of the most important but difficult jobs of a remote leader is building up the trust of your team to the point that they trust you to give them the information they need to get their jobs done well and to achieve their personal growth goals. This all starts with the leader. Over time, if you prove to your team that you have their best interest at heart and are serving them, they will trust that you will provide helpful information when appropriate and necessary. Sharing some information won't help the team or company become better.

Encourage Work-Life Balance

This is one of the most difficult things to do in a remote environment; however, there are amazing opportunities to have an amazing work-life balance while working from home, so we will spend a bit more time on this one. When I speak to executives about leading remote teams and themselves, I highlight four pillars of holistic health they need to consider for their employees and themselves. These pillars are mental, emotional, physical, and relational health.

1) **Mental Health:** Remote work can blur the lines between being at home and being at work. The Integrated Benefits Institute (IBI) conducted a study and found that 40 percent of remote workers and 38 percent of hybrid workers reported to have symptoms of depression.[10] We covered how important it is to maintain our mental health as leaders; however, when it comes to remote working environments, the chances of mental health decline are statistically higher than in-person working environments. As leaders, we have to take care of our mental health, whether seeking counseling, finding a co-working space to be with other people, or creating

---

[10] SHRM: A Potential Downside to Remote Work? Higher Rates of Depression: https://www.shrm.org/topics-tools/news/benefits-compensation/potential-downside-to-remote-work-higher-rates-depression

working hours where there is a hard out of the mental workspace. If leaders can communicate their mental health plan to their people, they will be more likely to create one of their own.

2) **Emotional Health:** Much like mental health, emotional health among remote and hybrid workers has been declining since 2021. The National Institute of Health defines emotional health as "the ability to successfully handle life's stresses and adapt to change and difficult times."[11] Emotional health is closely related to mental health but has one clear difference. Emotional stressors that affect emotional health are often things that catch us off guard and instigate an emotional response. These responses can be joy, anger, sadness, worry, or any other emotion on the spectrum. One of the ways that I can keep tabs on my emotional health is through mindfulness exercises. These can be breathing exercises, meditation, prayer, or anything you can do when you respond emotionally to a situation. Take some time, work through and with the emotion, and move forward with clarity.

3) **Physical Health:** This pillar is important yet complicated when working from home. On one hand, we can work from the gym or create an environment at home where physical activity is easily accessible. I encourage my team to take our team calls while moving, either on a walk, bike, treadmill, or stretching. On the other hand, remote work can suck us into our computer screens. I've had days where I wake up and head into my home office, and the next thing I know, I have 1,500 steps in, and it's dinner time. With nobody to break me away

---

[11] National Institute of Health: Emotional Wellness Toolkit (2022)

from my screen, I tend to get lost in tasks. Physical activity plays a significant part in our ability to handle emotional stressors as well as our ability to improve our mental health. As a leader, encourage your people to get up and get outside, as long as it's not snowing. Heck, even if it is snowing, cold temperature therapy is also a great way to push through the rest of your day. Get up, get moving, and create an environment where taking calls on a treadmill is commonplace.

4) **Relational Health:** Once again, remote work can be very lonely. If you take away computers, phones, and tablets, we would all look like crazy people talking into the air for eight to ten hours a day. Loneliness is a leading cause of declining mental, emotional, and physical health. Leaders, encourage your people to go into the office every now and then, if possible. Statistics are overwhelmingly in favor of human interaction over remote interaction. Dopamine and several other "feel good" chemicals are released in the brain when you interact with someone in person rather than online. Encourage your people to build relationships.

Establish Personal Boundaries

Finally, by establishing boundaries for yourself, you give your team permission to set boundaries for themselves. Make it clear that you are going on PTO, have a doctor's appointment, or go outside for a bit to throw the ball around with your kids. Remote work offers us amazing opportunities to live our lives while we work. If you are taking advantage of them, your team will, too.

The storms of remote and hybrid work can beat us down. They are innately lonely and can wreak havoc on our holistic health. As leaders, we have to be even more intentional with communication, collaboration, innovation, priorities, and structure, or our team will get lost in the storm. While the few years of the global pandemic were devastating, there's another storm we haven't yet talked about, and it may be more applicable now than we know. I'm talking about the crash of 2008 when our economy tanked, businesses closed, and people lost their homes. I was fortunate enough to be an active-duty Marine in Iraq in 2008, and as weird as that sounds, I wouldn't have wanted to be anywhere else during that time. Our next storm brings us to the foothills of 2008 when this devastating storm changed the life of a successful business owner in more ways than you think.

10

THE STORM OF RADICAL COMMITMENT: THRIVING THROUGH THE CRASH OF 2008

As we recover from the storm of remote work, over the horizon comes the final storm that we will plow through together. Our herd is intact, well-fed, and ready to move out, but this next storm is unpredictable. It's unclear whether it's rain, snow, massive winds, or softball-sized hail. What we do know is that we are a herd that has been through this before. We can feel the crisp change in the air and are ready for the next challenge. The herd is motivated and radically committed.

Radical commitment is a term that means several different yet unquestionably connected things. Radical commitment, in the context of leadership, is the idea that a leader is absolutely and unshakingly committed to doing what they say they will do. Some may say this isn't a storm; it's just the way leaders should operate, and this is true. However, what happens when unexpected tragedy or circumstances force you to test your commitment to your business, people, outside relationships, and even your family?

This was the storm that Greg Gast faced as the economy began to crash in 2006, culminating in the historic economic crash of 2007–2009. Greg had built an incredible human resource (HR) outsourcing business that was thriving with dozens of well-paid employees and more opportunities than his team could take on. Greg was (and still is) married with three beautiful children. This is Greg's story about the storm he plowed through by leading in a radically committed way to ensure the success of the most critical areas of his life: his family, his business, and his holistic health.

Greg's story starts in the late 1980s and early 1990s. As a motivated serial entrepreneur, Greg had been a parole officer, roofer, HR professional, bodybuilder, security guard, and almost anything else you could think of to help others and support his family. He was a driven entrepreneur looking for a professional spot where he could thrive and use his talents, skills, and abilities to maximize his impact on the world. He found himself in the healthcare industry working as an HR professional when he felt like he found his place. He loved the processes, procedures, and systems that made organizations thrive. While some may disagree with me, human resources make an organization run smoothly and, most importantly, legally. He loved the field but didn't necessarily love working for someone else. He wanted to be in control of his destiny. He wanted to control the wins and losses and eliminate the ceiling of working toward someone else's vision. After all, if you aren't working toward your vision, you are contributing to someone else. In 1998, Greg left his current company to open his own HR firm, Granatt HR.

> I was in my early forties at the time with a young family of three children, so I was unsure how to leap from a corporate paycheck to an independent consultant, but God blessed me with a unique chance to make that transition

from my job as vice president of HR at a healthcare firm to owner and principal of Granatt HR. Sudden changes in government payments for home care services resulted in the need for dramatic cost reductions for our company. After some thought, I proposed to the executive team that they outsource their HR services to me, promising a savings of over $100,000 annually (decent money in 1998). They agreed; we signed a contract, and all at once, I had a guaranteed income and four employees. My one caveat with the company was that if this worked, they would introduce me to other home health leaders for whom I could provide similar services. They did, and soon, I had client number two (sometimes the toughest client to get is that second one), and I had to hire more staff.

Now, leaving a stable career to start your own company could be an entire book of storms in and of itself. Greg knew that he would have to make commitments—to himself, his family, and his investors. He was committed to supporting his wife and children and creating a successful HR company. He was highly deliberate in creating guidelines around these commitments, including having a tough conversation with Nancy, his wife, about putting up their home as collateral for the business loan that allowed Granatt to become a reality. He was all in, and so was his family.

From 1998 to 2005, Greg built a multi-million-dollar company and a strong family life. While none of us did everything perfectly, and Greg was no exception, he honored his commitments well. Granatt grew mainly in the eastern Pennsylvania, New Jersey, and Delaware regions. Greg committed to his family that he would do his best to eliminate overnight travel, so he kept his client base close to home. Granatt's start was humble, much like many other startups. Greg and a few of his trusted staff met in his living room every day and worked out of their cars for the first year or so. They were working and prospecting all at once, trying to fill that pipeline of business that would eventually turn into revenue. Eventually, their hard work and grind would pay off. They would become a trusted HR partner to some of the East Coast's largest companies and were beginning to thrive. As Greg likes to say, "The phone finally started ringing the other way, where I was on the answering end."

Greg and his staff eventually moved from his living room to several office spaces in the Philadelphia region. Granatt had grown to twenty full-time employees. Greg wanted to stay away from independent contractors. It was nothing against them; they were independent contractors for other companies in all respects, but he wanted to build a workplace that people could rely on to pay their bills and that clients could depend on to provide consistent, high-quality services. Greg recalled, "Having other people depend on you for their livelihood, not to mention my mortgage payments and college tuition, is hugely stressful yet highly motivating. It required me to learn new things, and most importantly, it forced me to get up and do the work that needed to be done to ensure that Granatt succeeded and my family was taken care of." In addition, Greg made the best business decision in his company's history, which was hiring Jeff Green, an experienced HR professional who eventually became a partner in the business. Everything was headed up and to the right, as they say in the board room. However, things were about to change dramatically.

In 2005, Granatt had outgrown the spaces they were in, requiring them to find a bigger pasture for their thriving buffalo to graze. There were blips on the economic radar that were concerning, but nothing would stop them from finding another space, and after a lengthy search, they found the perfect spot. There were board rooms, offices, cubicle space, and plenty of window space. It was the perfect spot, but then the blips on the economic radar turned into dramatic spikes. For the next year, Granat began to see a steady decline in revenue and a dramatic decline in the American economy. In 2006, a recession was all but inevitable. Business was steadily declining, but the bills continued to pour in. They had just signed a three-year lease on a brand-new space, and the money was running out. Greg's commitment to his professional dream and to his family was about to be tested. Lightning began to crack over the mountains, and the herd was getting anxious.

In late 2006, as Greg was trying to figure out what he was going to do, the economy was beginning to spiral downward, and his clients were cutting out businesses like his as their first course of action. Other companies were beginning to close their doors, leaving people without work and crushing the dreams of entrepreneurs everywhere. Greg, however, was committed to keeping the doors open, and as he blazed through this commitment storm, fate would step in.

Greg, being the hustler he is, attended any event he could, speaking to anyone who would listen about Granatt HR. At one of these events, Greg and Jeff met the owners of a payroll service provider, Professional Payroll Solutions. They talked about the economy and the state of the HR industry. There was an immediate connection, and it just so happened that PPS was looking for a new space for their team. Greg and Jeff left the meeting knowing something needed to happen between the two companies. Greg had a building he couldn't keep paying for, and PPS needed a building to call home; it was a match made in chaos. Greg extended the invitation, and PPS quickly moved in, adding people to the space and, most importantly, sharing the rent.

In late 2006, Granatt HR took this relationship to the next level and formed a joint venture with Professional Payroll Solutions to form PROXUS LLC, a full-service payroll and human resources management firm. The organizations would combine their human resource powers to create something new that would save Greg from breaking the lease on the building and provide referrals and revenue to both partners. The only stipulation PPS had was that his people got first rights to the office spaces with the best window views. This partnership would save them from the first hurricane to hit, but like I said before, there's always another storm on the horizon. With the economy in full decline, Greg felt the pressure of his commitments.

The 2007–2009 financial crisis, often referred to as the Global Financial Crisis (GFC), was caused by a combination of factors, leading to a severe worldwide economic downturn. In the early 2000s, housing prices in the US rose rapidly, fueled by low interest rates and relaxed lending standards. This created a housing bubble, as more people bought homes, often using subprime mortgages (loans to borrowers with poor credit histories). Banks and financial institutions bundled these risky subprime mortgages into complex financial products called mortgage-backed securities (MBS) and collateralized debt obligations (CDOs). These securities were sold to investors worldwide, spreading the risk. When housing prices began to decline in 2006, many homeowners found themselves with mortgages higher than the value of their homes. This led to a surge in mortgage defaults and foreclosures. The rising defaults caused significant losses for banks and financial institutions holding MBS and CDOs. Major investment banks collapsed, while others were acquired to prevent failure. As financial institutions faced massive losses, credit availability dried up, leading to a liquidity crisis. Banks became unwilling to lend to each other, further exacerbating the financial instability. This crippled the US financial economy, causing the worst economic downturn since The Great Depression.

In 2008, PROXUS LLC was at the height of its decline. In the earlier days of Granatt's success, they had onboarded numerous temporary staff members who handled many small businesses' day-to-day human resource functions. In 2009, all these employees were let go, resulting in a major blow to the bottom line. Greg went for extended periods without pay to ensure their staff never missed a paycheck, eventually going over a quarter million dollars in debt. The business was, at best, trickling in; times were tough and seemingly getting worse. Greg's home life was suffering, and this recession storm had no end in sight. Greg recalled, "As the financial crisis of 2008 unfolded, I remember the uncertainty gripping our team. Each day was a challenge, but it taught us resilience and adaptability in ways we never anticipated."

Sometimes, storms can either come one right after another, or multiple storms can hit you at once. Greg was committed to his family but had difficulty figuring out how to be emotionally supportive when he walked back through the doors of his home after a long day of work. He would come home to his wife tired and beat, with his mind still on his commitment to keeping his business afloat. At this time, their kids were all college-age and out of the house, but Greg wanted to be present and committed to them as much as possible. Greg and his wife, Nancy, were committed to each other and knew nothing could break up their marriage, but they would have to put in very intentional work to ensure they remained on the same page. Often, they slipped off the rails, as those of us who are married tend to do, but they were committed to each other and Greg's business—after all, their house was still on the line.

Greg muscled through the thick snow that was 2008 and 2009, and the economy slowly began to recover. Each step forward seemed to get easier and easier—for both his marriage and business. Government assistance began to relieve the pressure on the global economy, and companies finally started crawling back to life. The phone started ringing again, and now, Greg had key partners equally committed to success to move into the future with.

Greg's many storms over the last few years could have broken him, but he was radically committed from the get-go. His commitment to building something great and maintaining a healthy marriage pulled him and what was now PROXUS LLC out of the storm and onto green pastures. When I asked Greg how he did it, he responded, "It may sound simplistic, but every day was focused on the slightest opportunity to increase revenue or reduce expenses, and each day started with an hour or more of examining every expense line and determining any chance to reduce the costs or delay the payments. The remainder of the day was spent expanding our current revenue sources with existing clients and looking for new business opportunities." When I asked about how he stayed committed to his marriage, he said, "I tried to solve our emotional issues with logical solutions, just like I did in the business. But that was the wrong approach. I needed to better listen to and understand all the emotions and situations frustrating Nancy—who patiently waited for me to work through the business troubles—rather than simply try to problem solve. I also agreed to engage in counseling to improve our communication. We slowly found our way forward together, working hard (especially for me) to balance my needs and respect Nancy's needs and desires. Of course, I'm still a work in progress."

ACTION STEPS

Greg braved the storm of being radically committed to the success of his business through one of the worst economic times in US history and to those who meant most to him: his family. Throughout my two decades of working with leaders, entrepreneurs, and executives, balancing these commitments is one of the toughest things those good leaders face. Often, leaders make an unfortunate choice: family *or* business. One of the many things we can learn from Greg's story is that, even through the hardest of times, being radically committed to both is not only possible, but it's also the key to surviving any storm. Let's break down how Greg stayed radically committed.

Sometimes, the Road we Take Becomes the Pathway to Something Else

Being radically committed doesn't mean things won't change. In fact, there is almost a 100 percent chance you will encounter massive amounts of change on your leadership journey. Being radically committed means that you are committed to adapting to change as it comes. Greg never dreamed that Granatt would one day merge with another HR company to create PROXUS LLC. It was a chance encounter at a conference that changed Greg's professional life and likely saved his company. Here's how to do that well.

- **Be Open to Change:** While staying committed to the overall vision, leaders must be open to adjusting strategies and tactics in response to new information, changing circumstances, and feedback.

- **Always Be Learning (ABL)**: Leaders who commit to lifelong learning will stay informed about the latest industry trends, technological advancements, and best practices. This helps them adapt to changes and make informed decisions.

- **Empowerment and Delegation:** By empowering team members and delegating responsibilities, leaders can create a more agile and responsive organization capable of withstanding storms like the 2007–2009 crash.

This also encourages innovation and flexibility within the team.

- **Resilience and Adaptability:** The buffalo has thick skin, making it one of the most resilient animals around. Developing resilience helps leaders stay committed even in the face of setbacks. Adaptability enables them to pivot when necessary without losing sight of their long-term objectives.

Being open to new opportunities and challenges helps create that sense of radical commitment; however, to take advantage of those opportunities, you have to be willing to be open to new possibilities or outcomes, and you must put yourself out there and make change happen.

Never Quit on an Uphill

This is a universal piece of advice we, as leaders, must embrace. If the lead buffalo stops moving, the entire herd stops moving. If the herd stops moving, it becomes increasingly vulnerable to predators and the storm itself. This is true in leadership and in life. This entire book has been about storms that leaders face and how to get through them. Leadership is hard; if I've said it once, I've said it a thousand times. There will be times when you want to give up and try something else I want to encourage you to stay the course. Don't quit when it gets hard, or you will never know if you quit because things got hard or it was truly not a good business fit. And, of course, you will miss out on the opportunities on the other side of the challenge.

This year, I completed a Spartan Race here in Colorado Springs (elevation, 6,000 feet above sea level). The Spartan Race I ran was a 13.1-mile race with over thirty obstacles spread throughout the course. I've run several of these races before, but this one was different. It almost broke me. The course was set up to encourage quitting in the middle. The beginning of the course was flat, and the obstacles were relatively straightforward. The walls were low, and the temperature was mild. However, as you reached miles four through six, the walls got higher, the temperature increased to a scorching level, and the hills got steeper. It took everything I had to stay in the game, including a friend to encourage me the entire way. I knew that I was radically committed to the race and was going to finish, but I wanted nothing more than to throw in the towel, head to my truck, turn on the air conditioning, and fall asleep. However, I was radically committed. There was no other option but to finish. After about mile ten or eleven, the hills got a little less steep, and the obstacles got a lot easier. I was able to pick up the pace a bit and enjoy the process along the way. Finally, we rounded one final corner and headed toward the finish line, where people were cheering and ringing cowbells as loud as they could. The final obstacle was jumping over a line of logs set on fire. I took one last deep breath, planted my back foot, and sprinted toward the logs, jumping as high and far as I could, safely landing on the other side. I finished the race. I wasn't setting any records, but I finished.

When we look at leadership and the challenges that leaders face, there will always be something to overcome—some storm to go through. If we know and understand this as a reality before we even step into these positions, we can commit to pushing through the hard stuff to get to the pastures on the other side. It is hard, but committing and sticking to your commitments will get you through anything you face. I'm *not* saying never to leave or quit anything. Sometimes, quitting a position or leaving a project is the right thing to do. I encourage you to stick to it through the hard parts and then decide to stay or go. Be radically committed to your teams, organizations, families, and, most of all, yourself.

Throughout our journey, from the battlefield to the boardroom, the storms we faced have underscored the importance of resilience, leadership, and adaptability. As we conclude, these themes weave together into a unified message: no matter the storm, the strength within and the support around us will guide us through any storm.

Final Thoughts from Greg Gast

There are many people who deserve acknowledgement for their contributions to the long-term success of Granatt/ PROXUS. First and foremost, I am deeply grateful to my wife Nancy for her willingness to support the plunge into founding and running a small business, while realizing (probably better than I did) the challenges to family and finances it would entail. Thankfully, she steadfastly managed more than her fair share of the family responsibilities while she was also working part-time. I very much appreciate the engagement of my children Traci, Ashley, and Travis who spent time working in the business, and effectively navigated many issues on their own when I may not have been physically or emotionally present.

Hiring Jeff Green was undoubtedly the best business decision I made. Initially as a senior level employee, then as a partner and eventually as the purchaser and CEO of the firm, Jeff's business skills and dynamic personality enabled the company to reach levels of success that would not have been otherwise possible. I continue to value our unique and long-standing friendship.

Finally, I will be forever grateful for the employees and clients who took a chance on engaging with this new HR consulting organization when we launched literally from my living room and the trunk of my car more than 20 years ago. You are all part of an American business success story. Thank you!

CONCLUSION

Like I said at the beginning of our journey, the storms we just walked through together were some of the most challenging storms life can throw at us, but here's another takeaway. As leaders, we have to be willing to do hard things. We have to be able to face the storms of life and leadership and say, "Let's get after it!" Throughout my life, I have seen the full spectrum of leadership and the implications of each side of that spectrum. I've seen poor leadership cost human lives and great leadership truly save lives. That's the scale we are working with here. Leaders, you have the power and influence to save lives, and I'm not just talking about combat. No matter the political, economic, or personal situation you find yourself in, I want you to step into leading. If you aren't in a "position" of leadership, lead even if you are afraid of the outcome because the stakes are too high.

According to the Centers for Disease Control (CDC) Morbidity and Mortality Report, the 2021 suicide rate among US persons of working age was approximately 33 percent higher than it was two decades ago, and the number continues to grow.[12] Unfortunately, this number is significantly higher for service members and first responders. While there are many

---

[12] Suicide Rates by Industry and Occupation — National Vital Statistics System, United States, 2021

explanations for these statistics, I can guarantee that there are people on this list who took their own lives because of an interaction with someone they saw as a leader. That is the kind of importance that needs to be placed on leading and leading well.

We began our journey by walking through the storms that come with leading teams in the Marine Corps, and while I know these storms don't pertain to everyone, there are lessons here that everyone can use to lead themselves and their people well.

- We walked through the massive storms of failure and how to overcome failure. Failure is the greatest teacher if we choose to learn from it.

- Then, we walked through the storms of leading from the front. Leaders, we *must* lead by example; we can't expect our people to do anything we won't do ourselves.

- The storms of success can force us to stop trying. When we succeed, we have to get ready for the next success, or it will turn quickly into failure. Celebrate well and move on.

- One of the most important leadership skills is taking care of and advocating for ourselves. The last military storm we plowed through was having the moral courage to know when you need to let others lead, which will save lives.

Our transition into the hurricanes and tornadoes of the business world led us into the wilderness of industry.

- Establishing and maintaining a healthy culture is the bedrock of organizational success. Establishing this early and often will ensure that you and your herd make it through the storm together.

- Bobby Mikulas and his team showed us that having a clear vision for the long game is more important than we think, and talking about our vision is even more important. I mean, who opened a hotel in the middle of the most devastating period in the history of the hospitality industry? Well, Bobby did!

- Finally, how do we maintain a high level of radical commitment that will take us through any crisis—even one of the worst economic periods of our country's history? Being radically committed to whatever you decide to pursue will keep you on track and accountable.

I want to thank you from the bottom of my heart for going through these storms with us. We are all better people, leaders, and followers because of the storms we went through, and I can promise you that if you learn from these resilient leaders, you will be able to thrive through any storm and live to see the next generation of leaders who have followed you continue to change the world. We're all leaders, followers, and influencers. Each of you has the power to make someone's life better. Lead with kindness, strength, influence, and power. Lead through the storm so you and your herd can rest up before the next one comes in. And always remember this: "Never quit on the uphill!"

HYBRID WORK IS TOUGH!

Discover how to lead any team, anywhere.

Go to ≫≫≫ jetlaunch.link/hybrid

ABOUT THE AUTHOR

My name is Dr. Travis Hearne. I am the founder and CEO of the Titanium Consulting Group (TCG), international best-selling author, globally sought-after keynote speaker, Marine Corps combat veteran, former intelligence officer for the Defense Intelligence Agency, cybersecurity industry expert, father, husband, and son.

My passion in life is to bring my military, academic, and professional experience to other leaders so we can walk through this leadership battlefield together. I've spoken to thousands of leaders around the globe, consulted with Fortune 500 companies, and helped executives and senior leaders change their professional and personal lives. My hope for this book is that you find better ways to lead your people and yourselves. We will *all* face storms in our lives; it's how we battle through them that counts. My mission is to enhance and empower leaders to become holistically healthy. What this means is that leaders are mentally, emotionally, spiritually, physically, and financially healthy. These five pillars of holistic health will ensure you are ready when opportunity strikes, and I'd love to walk with you through the storm of achieving this level of health.

Reach out to me at thearne@mytitaniumlc.com or find me on LinkedIn at www.linkedin.com/in/travishearne, on Instagram at @travis.hearne, or through my website www.drthearne.com. Let's learn to brave these storms together as one herd!

ACKNOWLEDGMENTS

To my amazing family. Traci, my wife, you continue to be the most patient, gracious, loving, and supportive best friend a guy could ask for. NONE of this could be possible without you and your tireless support to keep our worlds running while I do all of these crazy things. You are my sanity check, my biggest cheerleader, my greatest giver of feedback, and a trusted advisor. Thank you for always being my main squeeze and the one I will always love to hang out with!

To my three sons, Braden, Michael, and Brice. Guys! You guys are the peanut butter to my jelly. You are world-changing leaders that will impact the lives of so many people. Your energy gives me the strength and motivation to have fun! I want you to keep doing hard things, keep being kind, keep working hard, and keep loving one another and everyone you meet!

To my father! Dad, you taught me so many things in life, but the one that crosses my mind most is "Never burn bridges." You are the kindest and most loving dad around. You have motivated me to become the man I am today and have always supported my every move, even the Marines Corps (eventually). Your kindness is one of the many attributes that will pass on from generation to generation of Hearne's to come.

To my sister, Sarah. You are one of the best at taking on storms. Your resilience through all that life has thrown at you has been an honor to witness, and I couldn't be prouder of the woman, friend, mother, sister, kick-ass entrepreneur, daughter, and everything else that you have become! Keep kicking ass and taking names. Mom would be so proud of the woman you are, and she is smiling down on us every day!

To my mom, who is reading this from heaven. (Yeah, this one is for me). Mom, thank you for teaching me the value of hard work and for always being the one I could confide in when things got tough. You were always in my corner and continue to be, even though you've been gone since 2020. I miss and think about you every day, and I smile, knowing that you are up there cheering me on and watching your grandkids grow.

To my Marine Corps brothers and sisters and the families of those who never made it home. You are the inspiration for this book and my life. Without you, I wouldn't have learned how to become a leader or have the guts to take on the challenge of writing this book. To the families of Jacob Leicht, Kevin Oratowski, Shane Martin, Tyler Hensley, Val Trujillo, Cameron Miles, James Boelke, Trevor Blaylock, Dominic Neal, and Giorgio Kirylo. You always have a family to lean on. The Marine Corps and the Marines within will always be there for you. Thank YOU for your service and sacrifice.

Finally, to all of you! If you are reading this book, you have made the choice to become a better leader. Thank you for taking the time to read this thing! Thank you for taking a chance on a knuckle-dragging Marine who decided to jot a few things down and release it to the world. These stories were re-told to the best of our memories. There may be some things that happened differently, but these are hard lessons learned that I'm so glad you get to learn from without going through them. Thank you from the bottom of my heart!